Finding Your Light

Healing from Within

Heaven is not separate from Earth. Spirit is not separate from the body. A human being is not separate from the earth. Heaven and earth exist within us.

—Deng Ming-Dao

There is no abandoning of samsara in order to achieve nirvana... realizing this inseparability is the key to attaining enlightenment.

—41st HH Sakya Trichen

Elizabeth Rinchen Wangmo

Global Book
Publishing

Finding Your Light
Elizabeth Rinchen Wangmo
©2022 Elizabeth Rinchen Wangmo. All rights reserved.

ISBN: 978-1-956193-36-7
Book Design & Publishing done by:
Global Book Publishing
www.globalbookpublishing.com

Disclaimer: The Publisher and the Authors make no representations or warranties with respect to the accuracy and completeness of this work and specially disclaim all warranties, including without limitation warranties of fitness for a particular purpose. No warranty may be created or extended by sales or promotional materials. The advice and strategies contain herein may not be suitable for every situation. This work is sold with the understanding that the Publisher is not engaged in rendering legal, accounting, or other professional services. If professional assistance is required, the services of a competent professional person should be sought. Neither the Publisher nor the Author shall be liable for the damages arising here from. The fact that an organization or website is referred to in this work as a citation or potential source of further information does not mean that the Author or the Publisher endorses the information the organization or the website may provide or recommendations it may make. Further, readers should be aware that internet websites listed in this work may have changed or disappeared between when this work was written and when it is used.

Dedication

With deepest gratitude, I dedicate this book to Susmita Dutta—who shines her light through her smile, humor, enthusiasm, and support—for helping to fulfill a little girl's prayers.

To David Johnson—whose beacon of light shines brightly—for giving me safe harbor, and like an old sea dog, has weathered many a storm with me. Loyal and true.

To H.H. Sakya Trichen, H.H. Sakya Trizin, H.E. Jetsun Kushok Luding, H.E. Dagmo Kusho Sakya, of the Sakya, Kagyu, Gelug, Nyingma, Shije and Chöd Rinpoches, Khenpos and Lamas, the entire Sakya family, friends, and sangha, near and far, who have been generous and gracious as I ventured to solve Buddha's riddle.
This book is my offering of thanks.

Blessings one and all!
Peace in Love ♥ Love Heals All

Table of Contents

Homage

Manifesting Bodhicitta

As a frayed, broken bit of fibrous sinew caught adrift
in the water's current
still holds that jewel of the divine spark within its being;
the primal knowing: to grow; to become; to fulfill.
So too, are all sentient beings endowed.
This desire; this prime directive reverberating
in harmony with the source of all our becoming.
To grasp upon the rare chance to fulfill
the divine desire requires the grounding that karma has lovingly
tended and laid down like a gardener's mulch.
So, as the bit of tuber becomes aware
of having ground,
opens in trust,
taking root in the receptive mud
that offers up itself to nourish and support.
Thus, a reed grows from the mud
reaching upwards toward the light, swaying
weathering all to break upon the water's surface
To open its lotus to the divine in adoration and fulfillment.
A true creative force manifesting in harmony.

As the lotus tuber does, so should we
take root in the muddy ground our karma
has prepared for each of us so that we might be nourished
and supported on our Path.
Sit in meditation and sway as gently as the Lotus.
Open up within to discover your divine spark
and with the hook of compassion, attach yourself in samsara to
manifest your gifts For the benefit of al! sentient beings.
You will be happy, fulfilled, and in harmony:
body, speech, mind.

One

Preliminaries

Dear Dr. Sodhi,

Namaste! I pray that this finds you and your families well and happy! I am writing to you for several purposes.

While under your care, you helped me to heal from so many life-long allergies and ailments that had always plagued me. Many of them may not have even been mentioned to you as a concern because I had believed them to have been a permanent condition of my body. Yet, when I received a Western diagnosis of diabetes that would require a statin drug, my intuition led me to your doors. I was nervous. I had no background knowledge of Ayurvedic medicine. But, the moment I stepped into your offices, I knew I had come to a place of healing.

I credit you wholeheartedly for saving my life and for giving me a quality of health I had not thought possible. The healing I received under your guidance and care, according to my Western physician, had turned me into a new person medically... I was like a 20+ rather than my age of 50+. I sing your praises whenever the opportunity to do so presents itself! I humbly offer you my deepest gratitude. I thank you and all the members of your team for your nurturing, healing care of this body and spirit of mine...

You may remember that at the time, I was also undergoing a powerful, transformative, spiritual awakening. My body was revealing to me the devastation that my past thoughts, emotions, and experiences have had on it. I was observing my own karma and the karma of my family through me. My sudden awakening—more accurately, my realignment—has resulted in a glorious new way of being, yet such a change is very disorienting for the uninitiated, like myself, who had no spiritual upbringing or related guidance. By helping me nurture and care for my body, I learned to listen to it. Ayurvedic medicine, herbs, panchakarma, yoga, and basic breath work are a means to ground and center oneself. This is a great gift you have given me. Thank you.

Do you recall me asking you if Tara was a Hindi goddess? At the time, you were kind enough to refer me to the Sakya Buddhists in Seattle: Tibetan Buddhists who recognize their female Buddha as Tara. This led me through another spiritual journey of discovery regarding my private meditation practices. You may or may not recall my last visit to your offices: I was joyously giving goodbyes that were meant to be for an absence of only a couple of months—I was setting forth on the first leg of my spiritual pilgrimage: a journey to India, through Nepal.

A year or so transpired thus, and I was days from purchasing airline tickets to Delhi, India, when COVID-19 shut our borders. The week before, I had just completed the second physical medical exam to ensure that I was in perfect health to travel to India. My plan was to stay for a few months. However, the next week, the same week that the pandemic hit our borders, my body suddenly seemed to break: I was bleeding heavily. It was under rather rushed circumstances that I began treatment for late-stage colorectal cancer. There was a deep concern that my body may not be strong enough for the treatment necessary. It looked probable that I would be required to have a permanent device to manage digestion. I was shocked! Utterly shocked! How could I have been in perfect health one week and the very next week feel miserable in every way?

When I shared my shock with my family, it was revealed that this disease was one that both my mother's family and my father's family had a history of.

I immediately recognized this! You had helped me to clear and heal the karmically damaged parts of my body, and blocked chakras that I had inflicted upon myself over this lifetime; now, my challenge was to heal this very deep-seated, ancient family karmic damage. Despite Western medicine's concern regarding my body's stamina; having healed my personal karmic damage meant that I was now spiritually stronger. I recognized this horrifying, life-altering diagnosis as an opportunity for me to perform spiritual purification through my meditation practices!

My recovery and healing have been seemingly miraculous to some around me but would be common sense to practitioners of Ayurvedic and Eastern medicine, of yoga and meditation. And, my healing and transformation have not been confined to myself alone. It has been a catalyst for so many positive changes in the lives of family and friends.

I also discovered my writing gift. This led to the unique opportunity to write a little book on my healing meditation as an offering to help anyone who might benefit from it. It will also be an introduction to Westerners of a non-dual perspective way of being within their day-to-day lives. And, most importantly to me, it will also give me the perfect opportunity to publicly recognize and thank you and the clinic.

Our daily lives are our spiritual lives, and as such, our transformation is always unfolding.

The Sodhi Family exemplifies this beautifully. Your family has been a shining example of living a healthy, holistic, spiritual life whereby one can thrive by manifesting one's gifts. So, please know that I will honor you within the book as I've written in this letter. So, part of the purpose of my letter was to bring you up to date and to announce my intentions. Since my book is all about our need for true healing self-care, there is no one else I would consider asking but you two. I pray that you will grant my request.

Respectfully yours...

Dear Dr. Hannah and Dr. Krane,

At the time I came under your care, I was undergoing a powerful, transformative, spiritual awakening. My body was revealing to me the devastation that my past thoughts, emotions, and experiences have had on it. I was observing my own karma and the karma of my family playing out through me. My spiritual awakening was a wonderful and glorious new way of being yet rather disorienting for an uninitiated Westerner like myself—someone who had no spiritual upbringing whatsoever.

I began to learn to listen to my body and use mediation for healing. I had so many lifelong ailments of one sort or another slowly disappear. I was discovering that attitude, perspective, and habits were the underlying causes. Lifestyle choices!

A year or so transpired thus, and I was days from purchasing airline tickets to Delhi, India, for the second leg of my spiritual pilgrimage when COVID-19 shut down our borders. The week before, I had just completed the second medical exam to ensure that I was in perfect health to travel to India. My plan was to stay for a few months. However, the next week—the same week that the pandemic hit our borders—my body suddenly seemed to break: I was bleeding heavily. It was under these rushed circumstances that I arrived at your offices to begin treatment for late-stage colorectal cancer. I was shocked! Utterly shocked! How can I have been in perfect health one week and the very next week, have the opposite be true?

When I shared my shock with my family, it was revealed that this disease was one that both my mother's family and my father's family had a history of this same form of cancer.

I immediately understood the importance of this! Despite your valid concerns regarding my body's stamina, I had faith. If I was able to eliminate lifelong pesky ailments I thought permanent by lifestyle and attitude changes, then the diagnosis of this horrifying cancer was to be the next challenge. I would have to heal deep-seated, ancient family karmic bodily damage. I would have to utilize my healing meditation practice to help the healing process while you battled the cancer that plagued my body. You would focus on the body, and I would focus on the spirit.

We are now fast approaching the two-year mark after my surgery. My recovery and healing have been seemingly miraculous to some around me. When these events occur in people's lives, it forever changes them and the people in their lives. My healing and transformation have been a catalyst for so many positive changes in the lives of my family and friends, sangha, and acquaintances. In addition, I have met so many talented, kind, and caring souls at SCCA and UW who exemplify dedicated lives of service to the health and well-being of others. So many of them shared with me how their own journeys. All of them were stories of individuals who chose to incorporate their spiritual beliefs and the compassion of others into healthcare work as a means to living a fully purposeful meaningful life, benefiting their own well-being and those of our society. It has been my deep privilege to have met real-life heroes!

Because I believe that our everyday lives are, in fact, our spiritual lives, I recognize the two of you, Dr. Hannan and Dr. Krane, as two women who exemplify this dedication and compassion. I hold you both in the highest regard and am especially grateful to you for not only saving my life by freeing me from cancer but for helping me to return fully to my full capabilities. Please know that I am deeply grateful to you and the whole medical team who played a role in my care.

Throughout these past couple of years, I discovered a voice through writing. This has led to a unique opportunity for me to write a little book on my healing meditation. It will also be an introduction to Westerns of a non-dual perspective of being within their day-to-day lives. And, even more importantly to me, it will give me the perfect opportunity to publicly recognize and thank you, Seattle Cancer Care Alliance, and University of Washington Medical Center.

Respectfully yours...

Dear Gen Pema Sherpa,

I know that I've stumbled over my words, trying to say so during Zoom class at some point or another, but I feel that it is time to take a moment and offer you a proper thank you. We met just as I was to begin cancer treatment, a couple of years ago. Just as the pandemic closed the borders of all our countries. I signed up for your dharma teaching of Shantideva's The Way of the Bodhisattva. I wanted to hear the dharma while I under took my greatest tonglen purification challenge yet... to defeat death again. My visualization was that I'd tether myself to the dharma teachings like a rope—And on the very topic of bodhichitta... my current endeavor. How timely! Of course, you didn't know of any of this.

I am horrified that I must have seemed the typical American. I showed up and point-blank told you that I wasn't there to learn the terminology... I only wanted to hear how the Buddhists describe the way I see the world. The patience you must have required! And then to discover that I could only confirm my understanding of the teaching through my heart... through poetry. The fact that you read and understood reflects the highest caliber of your education. You actually understood me!

You did not know that you had become the oarsman to my safety raft... to traverse very difficult, deep-seated, family-karma waters. This purification challenge scared me. This would require that I reach for a love so deep and powerful that it could fill all want of forgiveness. Phew, to do that and then be able to meet Mahakala again in the flames and come back again to tell the tale!?! Yet, here I am. But, not by my own efforts or mind. Which brings us back to earth...

At the time, I told the whole class that one is never alone... unless they chose to be as much.

Your Zoom dharma teachings, your instruction, and all of those I met through the classes have provided me with their presence and support during a difficult time. True sangha. The energy of those with whom we spend time has such an impact on us and our well-being. You gave me the healing words of the Buddha and did an amazing job presenting Buddhist views on non-duality and emptiness. I was delighted by so much that I heard. And surprised to finally understand how my view differs from those of the highest minds. You helped me to discover what was so unique about my being. I bow low in deep gratitude. Thank you for being such a great oarsman!

Because of your great forbearance and tutelage, I wanted to thank you in a way to help demonstrate how interconnected we are, in ways we have no way of knowing. A beautiful mindfulness mandala to behold!

I will include some portion of this email within the beginning of my little healing meditation book, to publicly thank you and the sangha and because you, well, Gen-la, you are part of my story... Many blessings to you!

Two

Grounding...

et me elaborate a little. Buddhism was one of the many philosophies—religions—that I had set aside long ago without a backwards glance. In this case, it proved to be for the simple reason that I did not agree that "life is suffering." I could see his point. Who wouldn't? However, I had a different view...

But, as the letters above indicated, I was undergoing a huge paradigm shift... a spiritual awakening. Having my home demolished, my personhood vanish into thin air, my livelihood completely evaporated, and my very existence threatened by a disease? It could happen to anyone, right? Or it took a damn lot of trouble to get my attention! So, when Buddha reappeared at this time, it seemed the perfect kind of ironic humor, given my predicament. So you think you don't believe that life is suffering? Well, now look at your life! Don't you believe it now? Aren't you suffering? Isn't this suffering? Geez, it seemed I was to answer this challenge! So…

Attending Gen Pema Sherpa's discourses, then, was to be for the sake of mental grounding—to take up the challenge to occupy my mind with Buddha's riddle and perform my meditation practices to keep my body and spirit together... you know, so I wouldn't want to leave this body full of excruciating pain. Besides, I've always been good at solving puzzles, so, I thought, Hey, I've nothing else going—haha—so I might as well... and, who knows, I might just discover why the Buddhists didn't see as I do. It proved simple really. I have deep regards for the Buddha. A most brilliant mind, yet...

What truly surprised me, though, was discovering just how unique my view was. I've written of this in Enlightened Tales; however, some of the results are the outpouring of this book. As you will soon see, I hold a rather long and broad perspective...

Thrëë

A Bëginning of Sorts

Only a few years ago, my curriculum vitae on LinkedIn would have reflected an accomplished woman whose corporate professional life demonstrated a commitment to issues of equality and diversity. After thirty-plus years, I turned my attention to creative pursuits that surprised and delighted me by blossoming into a small business. Perfect, right? Well, not exactly. Just as I was beginning to get in touch with my creative, "feminine" side, the heavens came crashing down.

To wit, a massive cedar came crashing down during a snowy winter's night shortly before the holidays. Right down the center of our home, splitting it in two. Power returned to us only months later. It would take several years to get a roof back over our heads. Although the tree was no longer nestled in the center of the house, we were wilderness camping in the dead of winter, under heavy snow and ice—so rare to the Pacific Northwest—for those months before the power was returned to our neck of the woods. We were eager to be back online after months and able to reconnect with the world. I remember anticipating the email exchanges I would have to have with my clients and customers... knowing that I had missed out on all holiday sales. However, when reading the seemingly endless unread emails, what unfolded was difficult for me to take in.

I discovered that I was no longer me. My identity had been stolen. My bank account, my livelihood, my business... everything compromised. Everything taken. Nothing left. I could no longer function in the world. I couldn't even say my name was my own. I was truly nobody.

Well, that was it, wasn't it? What can one do? When the world takes everything from you, strips you of your identity, and you literally cannot participate in it, then what? What would you have done? What could you do?

Well, first I cinched up my coat and walked out into the snow. I simply started walking as I had as a child. The plan? None. I was done. Through. So, I guess the plan was to just walk until I couldn't anymore. Just as I had done before throughout my life. It is a very spiritually grounding form of meditation. At least Mother Earth did not reject me. However, this time, my heart was quite broken. Where would I go? There was nowhere "out there" for me to "be."

I realized that it was time to go inward. I sat in a tree to have a good, long think. There was nothing else for me to do. I began to meditate. Well, midway through my spiritual transformation, I'd received a shock that nearly took my breath away permanently! Among all the turmoil of my earthly plight, I'd been diagnosed with a late-stage form of hereditary colorectal cancer... that could be traced to the histories of both sides of the family. This time, it was my very root chakra of belonging in this world that was broken within my physical body.

It couldn't have been more obvious: my presence in the world, in society was no more... I had no belonging, I was no one; my body was heavily damaged and diseased at the very foundational core level, revealing blocked energy of Qi and of emotions at the critical first, root chakra of knowing one's belonging in this world Wow! Broken of mind, body, and spirit. A pain in the colorectal arse, for sure!

Needless to say, this kind of thing tends to give a girl a serious complex! I don't think I'm being a drama queen, here, do you? These signs were a wake-up call. I needed to listen. I had more thinking to do! More healing was needed. What would you do? How would you find the strength and willpower to keep trying? My walking this beautiful earth had led me nowhere, so I returned to the nook of the big-leaf maple tree... and kept to my meditations...

...then a funny thing happened.

It took me these past couple of years to fully comprehend my being-ness. It was more like remembering, and for me personally, it really came down to wrapping my head around the fact that I actually do see the world non-dually, not dualistically at all!

I was discovering that my "suffering" came from trying to adopt the generally accepted way of acting out in the world... from a dualistic perspective. Don't misunderstand me. I was successful in my civic and corporate life. It provided me with a purposeful, meaningful livelihood, so how could that be suffering?

I was shocked. What I thought that made me unique was my empathic abilities and the means of my healing for myself and others, but they proved to be the natural gifts that resulted in my way of perceiving the world... not the other way around! I hadn't quite realized until now that it was my perspective that made me unique. Spiritual aspirants meditate to achieve non-duality. My realization was to finally realize that my sight was what others aspired for themselves. The very aptitude that I most hid away—that I tried to stop myself from manifesting—was, in fact, the gift others sought.

I can only speak of what I know and experience. There are no coincidences. With this profound realization and plot twist, so much of my life fell open before me... and I understood. Not only for myself, but I now knew that I could help guide others to connect the proverbial dots—to heal their hearts and free themselves. You see, I'm not any different than you are. I remembered who I was and my natural way of seeing and understanding the world. I want to help you to remember too. Having spent a lifetime silent, the question became: how?

At some point in the midst of all this upheaval, I had to go to court to acquire a new name and identity. Having taken up the task of solving the Buddha's riddle, I had received a few dharma names. I sought to honor all of these new names, but the judge ruled otherwise. Too many! For several years, I had none, and now

I possessed too many. A delightful irony. The name that had been set aside by the judge was the name of a historically significant queen of former Tibet who personally ensured the publication of so many of the Buddha's teachings and sutras that were used throughout the country. So, to honor such an auspicious personage, I began to write and post pieces on social media.

As if in response to my prayers, I got an offer to write this book and a last-minute invite from friends to housesit their quiet, wooded homestead. A perfect setting to meditate and listen... and write. It was in the first days there that I stopped at their local grocers for foodstuff. Next door was one of those thrift/junk shops. Of course, I went in! And, sitting on the counter, as pretty as you please, was a bronze statue of Tara, of seven eyes, the female Buddha of Tibetan Buddhism. I couldn't help but laugh. Tara's appearance was an auspicious sign.

Crossing my path in this most unlikely of places seemed too obvious a sign even to the skeptic in me. The female Buddha of compassion, health, well-being, long-life, prosperity... well, there are twenty-one celebrated aspects, but nonetheless, here she was as an answer, to help me cut through all this knowingness of the human family and write a text that would help others to recognize and see the nothingness of fear and anger as I do, and thus begin a healing by learning to love ourselves.

So, Tara has accompanied me and presided over the writing of this guide. Yet, it is not really a Tibetan Buddhist text or instruction in buddhism. It is an active form of healing meditation practice. This means that the reader should compel their heart to acquire the healing capacity within this book. This is a different kind of spiritual learning, which involves communicating with the heart, not the mind. This is not a mind-only practice. That route is congested with so much knowing-ness and conceptualization... and a dearth of understanding.

Let me share with you a few of my insights and compel your heart to travel through this little meditation practice with me. I want to help you remember yourself. I want to show you how to free yourself from what hurts you inside. To be so happy that you radiate your light. There is another way of being: one where you can heal body and spirit... actually be happier, healthier... and discover who you truly are! If there is one thing I can guarantee, it's that you really don't know yourself at all... so, let's find your Light within...

Part 1

Cosmology – Our Body

Four

Looking in All the Wrong Places

Is it actually possible to live a spiritually fulfilling, happy, healthy, balanced life? Can one engage in life mindfully present, as your authentic self, and be responsive to life with intention, compassion, and purpose... on your terms?

Yes, absolutely!

Does life often overwhelm, stress, and exhaust you? Does it seem that all your energy is spent responding to its constant demands? Ever have that sense that you're going in circles?

Do you engage in spiritual practice? Are you doing "all the right things" but still stuck with relationship difficulties that are painful and all too uncomfortably familiar to similar experiences in the past?

Maybe you've previously sought out the advice of knowledge gurus about meditation, spirituality, stress, relationships, nutrition, exercise, goal-setting, and the like, all in your search to uncover the secret that will transform your life. You gained valuable information and insight but were the benefits short-lived? Did the recommendations prove impractical, ultimately competing for your time and energy in your already stressed, hectic life?

So, why is a calm, contented life so elusive?

Well, let's begin with the first and simplest reason. Let us begin at the very beginning: motivation... our intentions; our objective. What is the real purpose?

Just think back. In every incident, haven't your efforts been motivated by wanting to fix You. Be honest. Haven't you, deep down, believed yourself lacking, deficient, inadequate in one way or another? Most people are unhappy with themselves, so you're not alone. The ever-expanding self-help market is proof of it. This proliferation also reflects limited utility because they, too, are designed to help you fix what's "wrong" with you. They suffer from the same (false) motivation as you do.

You may be miserable, in a dead-end job, confused by broken relationships, suffering from any number of physical ailments or limitations... so, of course, it only makes sense that improving one's life begins with figuring out what's wrong with yourself and fix it, stat! Right? Or not? I mean, isn't it like changing a leopard's spots, after all?

I know, I know. I'm debunking the approach that has always existed, the world over. Unfortunately, it hasn't really worked, though, has it? Worse yet, the methods and techniques you receive from many of these self-proclaimed "knowledge gurus" are designed through promoting discipline and control over oneself and outward conditions and conduct in order to bring about the desired improvements. Fix the outside first. Fake it till you make it. Something of the old idiom about dressing the pig in pearls comes to mind. These efforts are not from a lack of sincere, well-meaning intentions. The trouble lies in our perspective of seeing from external appearances and conditions. Control is strictly in the purview of the ego. The ego is the disciplinarian, and the ego does not reside within your heart.

It was the ego that told you that you were inadequate. It is truly one's own worst enemy. In fact, everyone is suffering from this same affliction—this faulty paradigm.

This fact is critically important, and it is key to fully comprehending the impact of this way of thinking and reacting to the challenges of our lives. Only by way of healthy motivation and inclusive perspective can one break away from hurtful, stressful patterns in their life and stop compounding them by attacking oneself over matters and features that may only be superficially masking the true source of discontent. That is what this book is about. In fact, you will actually heal your body and soul! Not via discipline and control but by learning to love yourself...

So breathe. Take a breath deep into your belly. Relax. This is a spiritual journey. You are about to learn how to truly love yourself while healing your body—your life. You'll learn to rekindle the Light that is always in your heart. We are not going to do it by attacking and dismantling you but, rather, through the process of dismantling and unpacking all that stuff you thought was you and all that the world said you were. Once on the other side of this book, you will begin to see the Light of your true being and begin your journey. No head trips! A spiritual journey into your heart to find yourself at its center.

Thank you for being present! You are about to discover who you truly are...

Remember, we are beginning by chipping away and dismantling what we think of ourselves... not to judge but to see through all that crap. To that end, use your insight and your heart... Let's begin!

Five

A Compass to Navigate

Down through the ages, from the voices of the holiest and wisest sages among us, we have received the counsel that to begin any endeavor, we must start from where we are at the moment. Simple.

Everything begins with that first step.

The elegance of this simple truth belies the unseen blind spot that few observe. Much like using a roadmap of Grants Pass, Oregon, to reach a designation that is located in Viola, Arkansas, your efforts to fulfill your endeavors, whatever they may be, will be hindered, or simply DOA because you misunderstood your initial location, thus throwing all calculations of distance and terrain out of whack. You end up using the wrong map. It is imperative to realize this central point.

If we are to begin where we are, then we must know where that is! To do this, we have to know something of our being that places us "where" we are. We need to know where we are evolutionarily. Only makes sense, right?

Through the course of our lives, we have acquired some conceptual understanding of how our universe exists and operates. The actual workings, the underlying mechanics of which are elegantly expressed through the language of inorganic and organic chemistry, of quantum physics; through equations and mathematics. All the beauty and symmetry of the expressions of life as we experience it, relies on the use of a reference point—a series of reference points to build upon.

Shakespeare wrote, "To thine own self be true." Or, as Socrates had put it: "Know thyself."

Our suffering tends to involve the over- or under-estimation of ourselves and the situations or circumstances we find ourselves in. Let me repeat this: you suffer when you overestimate or underestimate yourself or the situation. Beginning with a faulty reference point distorts and colors how we see and understand our circumstances. Our view, our perspective, and where we "think" we are, prove to be a faulty calculus built on incorrect assumptions and prejudices. It's no wonder our endeavors go sideways and the results of our effort goes off the mark.

We already recognize this in our lives. We experience this all the time! Almost always without a thought. So-called "fate" mocks us when our efforts fail us and our hopes have fallen apart. Worse yet, it seems that only after things have gone disastrously wrong, we are given a glimmer of insight into our errors in judgment. Unfortunately, for all of us, it is in our hubris and forgetfulness that we continually rely on concepts, notions, and schemes we've devised and revised for ourselves that are far grander, far more elegant or complicated and certainly far more aligned with our preferred plans, beliefs, or prejudices. This only eschews and limits our efforts, compounding and muddling and confusing us... making it even more difficult to know where we are, much less which way will bring us through.

What's worse is this reliance on our variable perceptions and catering our responses in life on a "situation-by-situation" basis, meaning we are constantly adjusting, recalibrating, and expending our energies like shifting sands. I know, this goes against the grain right now. Businesses often tout a core tenant to stay fluid and responsive, and we expect the same of ourselves, in this 24/7 world. Such shifting sands means that we are not truly aware of where we are... or what we are, for that matter, making ourselves a very unstable, unreliable reference point. A compass without true north to navigate from.

This is the human blind spot! Our blind spot. Your blind spot. We need to recognize and acknowledge it. No wonder we got lost and continually lose our bearings.

All is not lost, however. That calculus we use? Even incorrectly, it shows us that it is a built-in mechanism that already operates within our nature. We already use it, instinctively, to navigate our daily lives. We don't have to learn any new skills! We just need to know ourselves better so we can become a more reliable reference point—a better compass for ourselves.

A compass that recognizes true north generates more accurate coordinates that we can use to navigate our lives. Gaining a better handle on what really drives our motivations, thoughts, emotions, and activities is of paramount importance to creating more accurate assessments and happier lives.

Your first purpose is to be your compass—your center.

We just discovered that we don't really know our own motivations, and worse, that we sabotage our endeavors by failing to recognize how our shifting view of self leads to misknowing ourselves, thus making things worse and confusing matters to the point where we become frustrated, throwing up our hands, and asking, "Where am I? How did my life end up here?" The good news is that we've uncovered our blind spot, providing us with some clue of the direction where we need to look...

Phew! I'll grab the shovel. It's time to dig in and get a closer look at how we, as humans, truly respond to the world—what truly motivates and underpins all those grand concepts and notions we devise for ourselves. It's time to find that collective beginning point, our true location on this map of life! Just sit and relax. I'll do the digging. Let's see what we uncover...

Six

Finding Ground

We humans have expressed and manifested our collective endeavors through civilizations of advanced societies, embellished with languages, cultures, laws, religions, sciences, and arts. We have inherited thousands of years of culminating knowledge on which we built the world we live in today. I do not know your individual knowledge base or how tightly you might hold onto certain beliefs and viewpoints. For this reason, it is important that I ensure that you and I are at the same spot so we can see the same view together. We need to be using the same map. Only then can we comfortably take this journey of discovery together without anyone getting lost.

And, to do this, we need to begin at... let me call it ground zero, in keeping with the previous metaphor. It doesn't get any more basic than looking at our human family genome and ourselves as members of the vast collective of sentient beings that inhabit this world. So, let's take a cursory peek at this collectively acknowledged "beginning"—our cosmology.

Whoa! Seems a bit far, doesn't it? Remember that calculus you use instinctively? Well, we have to go this far back to see most clearly... gain an accurate line-of-sight, as they say. We will discover that our biological building blocks hold the key that unlocks our ability to see all that we already know.

All that is of this universe, from that initial spark to how we experience it, follows a very primal principle It's a principle taught to us in school, about the three propensities, or properties from which all of our existence has been built. The properties and nature of light.

All things operate from this basic building structure. Three elementals: a positive, a negative, and a neutral. Or, you might say: an active charge, a receptive charge, and the static charge. You might recall the images used in grade school science class about the subatomic particles: electron, proton, neutron. The static charge is the union of the two charges interlocked. The appearance of these merged charged particles would appear stationary to an outside observer. Their energies bind them together, their centers stabilize them, and they're seemingly less volatile than the dynamic free radicals of the positive/active and the negative/receptive charges. This stationary state is density: the seed of all manifested things, of matter... of earth and of life.

Try to visualize these energy elementals, not as in the science class diagram of being "contained" within an atom but the way in which they potentially interact. The positive is always active, "seeking", drawing nearer; the negative is always receptive, "repelling", withdrawing; and the balanced energy of two opposing particles (positive and negative) is "held" together in seeming equilibrium in a dynamic, powerful embrace. Visualize and be mindful of this concept while reading on. What follows will be descriptions of everyday human activity that we are familiar with for the purpose of letting you see more clearly how these elemental energies play out in our world.

Everything, absolutely everything in this realm, as we experience it, operates on and is built from this simple coding. The simplest, most basic of building blocks, this simple calculus created all of space, including the sun and moon, the rocks, weather, garden vegetables, peonies, the fjords of Norway, and even your attitude. It is all energy in its full manifestation.

The same calculus allowed us to formulate all that we have conceived. From the gods, ethics, governance, wars, civilizations, and environments we create to live in, to homemade bread, cheese and champagne, to our very emotions... all of it is built or expressed through this clunky, simple attract/repel/binding mechanism.

Our ability to breathe, see, hear, touch, taste, and smell... the very means by which we can even "know" we exist—it took aeons for this simple set of coordinates, this clunky calculus, to become a means of perception, of senses, of smells, and so on. Just try to fathom the impossibility of this miraculous feat! I am awed, and so should we all be. Forgetting ourselves, we lose sight of how amazing it is to just have this opportunity to experience being! And it's deeply humbling to realize that no matter how grand or elaborate our minds are able to construct or conceive, all of it is only possible through the energies that attract/repel/bind... the energies of Light. Brilliant!

Let me elaborate a little further to help us get our bearings before moving forward...

Emptinëss – Hër Physics

Since our beginnings,
we humans have held sacred
the trinity of things ethereal and material.
Yet, it too dissolves
recognize the emptiness at its center—
merely an axis for the turning.
This axis, this fourth thing of the nothingness,
possess energy of abiding genesis—to be and not be—
yet ground so all else might reach fruition.
She's the space she dances; men can't observe.
She unites their field theory—
the enigma that perplex
man-made gods in plain sight.
With each virtue, the afflictions: pride, envy, and rivalry.
Seemingly impossible odds.
They create within her very being indigestion.
All that hot air!
The blah-blah-blah of ego talking
under its own dualistic delusions
agitating the balance of all things ...
turning the trinity that turns the wheel.
Yang exhausts; Yin rises.

The primal force of equanimity.
She dances amidst her three suitors.
Fathom a world of being where three reveal
the fourth: the everything in nothingness.
In All.
Our Being.

Sẽvẽn

Emotional Storms

T his switching mechanism, which is the attract/repel/bind calculus, represents the three propensities of possibility. Contained within it is the dynamic tension, or energy, that is self-activating at all times. It never stops. Always is. Always generating. All things become and dissolve through this prism of becoming... of being a living sentient being. We are of the nature of Light.

So the primary directive contained within this calculus is to seek balance. It's the movement of seeking out, of grasping, and of adhesion to bind together or to repel, creating the dynamic pulling inward movement. Internally, this signaling to seek, repel, or absorb is quite powerful. It created the universe, after all! Most of this activity within our bodies occurs naturally in balance, all attributed to this calculus, but when you and I begin to decide that we know better and choose which signals we want to attend to or not—or when we misunderstand the signals—then we begin to interfere and disrupt the entire balance of our ecosystem, our homeostasis.

One of the "disadvantages" of being human—highly advanced sentient beings—is that we get involved in interpreting our energies. The ego, more specifically. As part of our biology, the mind is the location where the engine of collecting signals, internally and externally, congregate and are interpreted, conclusions made and then redirected. When the ego gets involved... well, it was designed to recognize your internal signaling, and by outwardly gathering the external stimuli of your senses, a cause or a salve is created. Emotionally, find a cause (a blameworthy object) or a salve (a means to resolve or satisfy). This process of signaling courses through our bodies and outwardly is present at all times. Through our nervous system and energy network is the highway that our electrical magnetic energy signals travel. Whenever we sense something is off-balance, our minds are always busy, trying to figure out what is wrong and what will rectify the problem.

The process of human development supports this process of seeking activity. As infants, our survival depends upon our parents. Food, shelter, warmth, and safety are all provided to us from external sources. We are dependent, vulnerable beings. As we grow and mature, we believe that we become independent, yet as we will see, our emotional nature developed as infants, so our ego's responses to imbalanced stressors remain quite infantile—dependent. We grow up, think for ourselves, and believe ourselves mature, yet we hold such a deeply embedded expectation that fulfillment will be met by forces beyond - outside of ourselves! This unspoken, unrecognized expectation, when left unmet, is extremely volatile. And it's the source of all of our woes.

The ego always identifies something to fill that perceived void! Always! I repeat: always! It is constantly grasping to fulfill its directive to devise an explanation and resolution for the tension, the discord, the imbalance within your body. Rightly or wrongly.

Rightly, you and your body respond accordingly to bring yourself back into balance. No imbalance. Centered.

Wrongly, you will only cause further imbalances and confusion, increasing the urgency and demand for reconciliation, for satisfaction... the seeds of fear and aggression.

This is the source of our emotional being. Please, sit with this for a moment.

This is the true source of our emotional being—the origin and seed of all of our emotions, which are nothing more than misdirected, misunderstood, suppressed energies that arose from deep within.

This is what has been mistakenly understood by our holy sages as desire. We cannot eliminate desire, so we must stop the guilt-shaming, stat! We need desire. Without this operating within... well, bluntly, we would be dead. The propaganda against desire simply reflects ignorance of our true nature and self-loathing to the highest degree. It only builds anger, in all its suppressed and repressed forms. It is the misplaced, misdirected, intercepted, misinterpreted perception of that desire that has led to eschewed motivations of greed, lust, wars, and all other sorts of mayhem throughout human history.

Our ego, not knowing how to resolve signaling, panics and works furiously to find something to quiet and resolve the signaling. You will "feel" that you "need" something or are "lacking" something. The ego seeks possible "objects" that might "satisfy"... and, as we are very well aware, whatever we have personally decided on that would satisfy, is usually only temporary. We've uncovered the wellspring!

Sadly, we believe these emotions are real and are based on what our minds/egos have perceived or devised for us. Retail therapy and so much of our consumer culture depend upon exploiting this basic human sense of "lacking"—of our constantly seeking out objects, experiences, etc., for fulfillment. It is rather humbling and maybe even embarrassing, I know. But, please remember, we need this ability to survive! This one example confirms how far we have distanced ourselves from actually knowing what would really make us happy. It's the same calculus—hijacked. And, admit it, whatever it was you wanted from your retail therapy had nothing to do with any real need... we'd long forgotten what that was all about if we ever knew to begin with. We were trying to fill a void. So, no shame or guilt, please—just acceptance.

Eight

❊

The Storm Within

To elaborate, consider an example where a biological signal alerts the mind of a nutrient deficiency, which continues to signal over time, easily becomes congested, changing the signaling into something that feels more like "unworthiness," being unloved, in addition to whatever bodily damage or disease the deficiency creates. How? Your ego-mind being inattentive or non-responsive to your body's requirements generates blocked, agitated energies and increased imbalances. The body is being neglected. It is stressed and imbalanced. Signaling! Constant neglect reflects the disparity between the body and mind—matter and energy. Such a failure to adequately provide your body loving self-care for its well-being and homeostasis signals a set-in lack of regard for yourself... a sense of worthlessness... the seed of depression, repressed anger, and illness.

Let me pause for a moment here to iterate that I am using broad strokes so you can grasp the true nature of our being: the dense, manifested physical bodies we inhabit and the energies (our energy bodies) that operate and flow through them and around them.

Unattended, ignored, or unresolved signals become stronger, and the longer this activity is sustained, the more energy that will become congested within. Over time, this kind of neglect results in all sorts of manifestations in our lives, but they all arise from the emotive energies we feel and express, especially those we suppress and repress. So much of this activity occurs in unawareness until we are diagnosed with one of the innumerable lifestyle diseases.

We comfort ourselves by saying that our disease is hereditary. That's no comfort! It actually reveals we have been responding to our life experiences in the very same exact manner as our parents and ancestors throughout the ages! Shocking... and humbling to know that maybe we haven't evolved as much as we thought! Your hereditary disease is a propensity. The severity of its manifestation developing in your particular body and affecting your life will be determined, in part, by how closely you, yourself, align your habits and your perceptions of the world with those of your family before you.

Your body will respond to stressors and deposit congested, stagnate energies in the same habitual pattern encoded within it... this is ancient karma, coded within the DNA. This disease propensity is the damage of blocked energy, of the coding that can no longer communicate effectively, garbling the signal through this area of the body because of longstanding neglect of the attract/repel/bind mechanism. And, remember, earlier when I described the activity of the merged particles as the origin of density, of matter? Well, keep that image in mind because within the body, where there is unresolved tension and built-up energies knotted up—that is density. You made that pain real now! It represents the seed of disease—of illness. And, as we well know, density's heaviness only draws more to it like water flowing to the lowliest point. A pain in the neck, indeed!

From this example, our closer look has opened our eyes wide. Our line of sight now reaches deep into our ancestry. The devastating effects of being inattentive to ourselves is the source of all the tension and conflicted energies; it's the source of all emotions... a primary source of disease and certainly the source of all our troubles and woes.

Well, so here we are, in the eye of the emotional storms that we have generated for ourselves. Inside and out. It stands as the source of fear, anger, worthlessness, disease, and who we think we are—all plainly observable, lying before us. We can see more easily that ignoring basic needs of self-care and self-love has devastated the entire human family throughout human history.

Shall I get us an umbrella? Or, a box of tissues? The good news? You and I have just gained our bearings...

We can see this and begin to reassess our understanding... our view... our perspective. We can recognize that our being is of two natures: energetic and physiological. We can clearly see the critical need for equilibrium between the energetic and manifested forms of our being.

Thë Body Politic

We are as one divided, yet becoming.
Scattered children of compassion—of Light.
We are here NOW
to accept our true being,
merge our dual natures;
of energy, of body—
to remember,
to discover who we truly are;
develop the treasure hidden within;
manifest them fulfilling your happiness
and for the benefit of all.

Collectively, as each of us takes up our true purpose,
we begin to transform and return our world
from one of sorrow, woe, and suffering
to one of loving-kindness, compassion, and harmony.

Choose to be happy and discover who you truly are.

Nine

The Eye of the Storm

I've led you right through to the center of all the turmoil and drama, where all the human suffering is manifesting and swirling around us. Pay dirt! This is the best vantage point. Ground zero.

The calm before emotions.

This space of calm is what all the spiritual aspirants seek to attain and abide in. This is the location where we can pivot to a healthier perspective and make more mindful choices. This is where we anchor ourselves and find our way to clear skies... to discover our authentic self and happiness. We can lighten our burdens by recognizing and accepting this truth about ourselves.

Motivation: We have looked closely at this all-too-human blindness to ourselves that leads to neglect, imbalances, disease, and projecting emotional stressors. We uncovered the hidden workings that run through all of us as the true underlying source that colors all of our motivations and intentions. We can see now that the old paradigm of finding what's wrong and fixing You is a matter of faulty motivation—one that causes increased imbalances and throws us further from our center.

Perspective: This led to the realization that the lack of loving self-care is the origin of all emotional energies, which led to another truth: our ego's intersession to interpret and keep us in homeostasis has made tragic errors in judgment by the constant looking outwardly for answers and solutions, thus distorting and confounding what may have been the real internal need. We had the wrong perspective—the wrong understanding.

Self-Love: And, then, the sad truth, which will take us time to accept and work through, is the realization that all that chasing after happiness means that we unknowingly gave ourselves much of our own trouble and woe, compounded by the guilt and shame of "wanting" that might have been associated with it. All of this outwardly directed activity made us moving targets. Chasing after happiness reveals that we have lost ourselves—lost our centers. It indicates that you have become a broken compass, unable to pinpoint the source of your true happiness. Discovering who we are will teach us how to love ourselves and how to be happy. Fantastic, right? So, are you ready to lighten up?

We can see that none of the hidden workings that drive the universe is personal to us individually... to you or to me or to any of us, for that matter! So, just stand right there and unpack all that guilt, shame, blame, fear, anger, frustration or whatever twisted hurt you've been carrying around inside of you and remove it! It's quite damaging to your body, damaging to your energies, and damaging to your spirit. So, dump it! It's distorting your perspective and weighing you down—holding you back.

While you're at it, unpack the dead-weight of resentment, bitterness, entitlement, and rage that you've carried around this world for so long; drop those negative feelings directed at parents, religion, society, government, relationships, and your body. The result of whatever occurred in the past is most certainly playing out in all of our lives in the here and now, but we have all contributed to this storm in one way or another. What's the point in wasting time trying to find someone to point the finger at? This is perpetuating the old paradigm. It never ends, and it never heals.

You only keep chasing and keep yourself off-center... lost. Holding onto the pain that you recognize as "yours" means you have made it your identity. What are you if not all that pain? I've brought you to ground zero to show you that you are now free to choose to drop this identity. This is not You. It never was. You can breathe deeply and choose a more positive, more authentic identity. Yourself.

We are all seekers, yes, but to seek to know ourselves means that we are willing to be accountable for our own well-being and happiness. If we aren't willing to do this for ourselves, then where in that primal calculus do you see how any one of us might put that expectation on anyone else? We each have to learn how to love ourselves and heal. So, give yourself a break... your first act of compassion. Love yourself enough to let that weight fall to the ground. Don't hold onto it within your body.

Doesn't that feel better?

Just look at how far we've come! We're light years ahead of most.

Just think of all those souls who've spent their lives in meditation, undergoing acts of self-denial, seeking this very same understanding. The old paradigm's methods contain within them that inherent battle that requires so much energy in pursuit of controlling the mind and disciplining the body, relying still on external factors. This analysis and sorting through all of those superficial masking conditions is vital, allowing us to more easily recognize secondary manifestations, showing us our failure so we can know and accept ourselves.

Many soulful persons have spent years in retreat, disengaged from life, seeking the understanding that we've just gained for ourselves. We know that we needn't bother playing the blame game or chasing after all that emotional drama because it's all merely distraction and not the true root of why we hurt and not in harmony... homeostasis.

And, don't forget all those offerings crowding the self-help shelves. Reaching for them with the wrong motivation, without internal reflection and understanding, will result in yet another frustrating effort to discipline and control yourself. Energies expended to fix or solve some such thing that you decided "needed" fixing so that you will become more acceptable to yourself... all so you can then be happy? This is self-loathing. This is not love.

This old paradigm proves rather unworkable and certainly limiting with respect to positive results, especially regarding healing both the body and spirit. The time commitment alone is daunting because you are battling with your very ego. Who's got that kind of time? I've just led us through a huge by-pass!

Ah, a glimmer of light! We're trying to manage hectic lives, after all. The perspective we just gained—this shortcut alone—is transformative.

Now, I know that all of this is so much easier said than done. Believe me, I know! We humans are notorious for convincing ourselves we're "over" some hurt. We intellectually write off all of our troubles, walking away from relationships and whatnot, believing it's all over and done with. Not so!

This returns us to that big blind spot that we all share. As we've come to learn, often what we thought we had made peace with from some past hurt didn't address the "real hurt" deep inside us. You dealt with the outward conditions and effects... and, well, let's face it, we typically rely on time to be our great healer, believing that with all the sundry distractions of everyday living and some distance, then overtime, we will begin to forget, thus lessening our pain. We've rationalized, we've let it go, and we expect time to heal while we bury it and afflict our bodies to carry the burden. This is not loving compassion.

We didn't heal. We just buried it deeper within ourselves, compacting yet another layer of secondary unresolved, blocked energy on top, masking the root cause yet again. We forgot to release it from and heal our bodies as well. And, it is this critical component that goes to the heart of the purpose of this book.

You see, I don't wish to offer you just another little meditation guide and send you on your way. I didn't write to expound on the flaws of the old paradigm. Nor did I write this to merely help you comprehend what you already know of your world and connect you to it. Or to help foster an acknowledgment of our place in this universe as sentient beings that cohabitate this beautiful, grand ecosystem we call the universe.

I actually want to free you from the old way of understanding who and what you think you are. So much of that is not You. Never was. I want to help you remember. Why? So that you will risk spending time with yourself in reflection long enough for your body to trust and open up—to release and heal. True loving self-care. To truly learn to know yourself. To love yourself. Only then will your world—my world, our world—can be transformed into a healthier, more loving, and more harmonious home where we and our planet can thrive!

In fact, reading this book is designed to be an experience of an active healing meditation practice.

Traditionally, active forms of meditation that incorporate visualization, chanting, dance, drumming, etc., are considered tantra. Yet, the term tantra has been so misused and misunderstood. Tantra in yoga and meditation refers to methods that help to harmonize one's body, energies, and mind within spiritual practice. I will use both active and tantric interchangeably. In fact, active forms of meditation were humans' first form, and are certainly the most effective form of meditation known. As were the first forms of worship. Many still are.

You are a physical entity, yes, but you are so much more. You are an energy source and an energy conduit. We are spiritual beings in manifested forms. Our "happiness" depends on homeostasis. Our bodies and spirit must be in relative harmony to be contented and healthy. From this state of being, all things flow. This is what I want for you: to remember that we are beings betwixt what is and what is not. We have agency to choose.

My wish for you is to love yourself, fully.

Let's face it: there really is no way around it! To dig out and release energy blocks, emotional pain, etc., requires self-reflection. This means meditation. I have helped to dismantle the underpinning of so much of what we think drives our efforts in this life. Even if we can now see that we simply didn't understand our true nature, we still hold all that emotional baggage we associate with it. We still hurt. We still believe this pain is our identity. Our lives are still just as they were before you started reading this book. We have to dig that hurt out of these precious physical bodies we are very fortunate enough to inhabit.

And to do this, we have to look at ourselves and recognize and name it. It is recognizing the truth that releases the pain, allowing healing to begin and providing us insight. So much of our true desire for harmony and balance—homeostasis—has been through the ages of our human social and spiritual development, subverted into myriad forms of hurtful experiences we recognize in our daily lives. I'm sharing with you the path I took to heal and transform my life completely.

With this more open, receptive willingness, we risk touching our wounds so we can clear and heal them. This risk is an act of love of the most divine. Entering into any self-reflection from your heart's wisdom ensures that your experience with meditation will be a path to discovery, forgiveness, and love. It will be deeper, more healing, and definitely more enriching because you know that you are simply going through the hurt, like a storm, to find that calm, the eye in all that turmoil, to finally find You. At your center, you will be making delightful and surprising discoveries about yourself that you did not remember. You will discover talents, skills, and abilities that have lain dormant within you all this time. You may not think that this could possibly be true right now, but you will.

...those unacknowledged, unrecognized talents that are You are your gifts to gain fulfillment and live the harmonious, prosperous life that was always meant to be yours.

Part 2

The World Within Us

Ten

Meditation Forms – Overview

I've led us through a grand sweep of the cosmos to show you that we are an organism, a sentient being of this universe and we came into being in the same manner and method as everything else. All of our features and processes are manifested by the same means. All of it is rather impersonal, yet all sentient beings' contentedness and harmony with the rest of existence depends upon this homeostasis of being. We call it "happiness." The primal directive. Everything else...? Just secondary considerations. If our perspective is correct, then our motivations and intentions will be as well. Our choices and endeavors will be harmonious, in accord with our truer desires, and we will be happy, healthy, and prosperous.

Looking through new eyes, we recognize that our body's natural processes to acquire and maintain homeostasis can, if unfulfilled, lead to imbalances that trigger the activation of our egos, creating the seeds of emotions as well as driving the stressing energy outward to seek resolution.

From this vantage point, we can now look in at our own personal afflictions. We will be able to more easily identify our true underlying wounds without getting lost, distracted, or caught up in the web of details (no offense, but you know, all that stuff that pisses us off, harms, or hurt us!) within any particular event that might have caused the wound. Remember, you may be able to resolve something to your satisfaction intellectually, but, until you've attended to healing the body as well, you've only suppressed the harm further, inviting it to re-emerge in some other form of "need" later.

So, the true purpose of meditation is to keep in touch with yourself... to listen. A simple daily self-care activity that lets you keep in touch with yourself, your true authentic self and needs... supporting your homeostasis, your happiness, and your well-being.

This book is a purification—a healing meditation practice in itself. An active form that you are now bravely attempting. Once through it, the simple suggested meditation practice I offer at the end will be one that is readily adaptive to incorporate into your life. It will be one that is responsive to both aspects of our true energetic and physical nature. But, first let me perform a little due diligence, providing a quick look at the basic meditation forms that have served our human family through the generations. Having done so, we will take a look at examples of our everyday conduct as a practice of purification: to recognize it and name it so we can then accept and lovingly forgive. No judging! We are looking at how we misuse our energies, so as to change for the better.

It's amazing how many meditation technique offerings there are these days. The vast offerings available are quite diverse and can be both overwhelming and confusing to sort through. However, regardless of whether it's the simple "five-minute" de-stressing meditation technique you find in a wellness magazine or one of the guided meditation apps on the market or some specialized form like sound therapy or one of the more physically engaged yoga practices (e.g.,Qigong Tai Chi, martial arts, dance or a walking regime), they all offer the opportunity to bring balance between the body and mind to varying degrees. All of these grew out of the more formalized and spiritual techniques found in ancient Hindi yogic, Buddhist, and Taoist meditation practices. The more modern forms like sound therapy seek to acknowledge and incorporate our energetic being as well. I strongly recommend making an active practice of performing the basic five Elements qigong movement routine before you begin any sitting meditation. I do. It is simple and extremely gentle yet profoundly effective. It will help you get back that primal connection that centers your energies, lets you once again feel and know that you reside in the heavens but are firmly grounded on earth.

How is it that a sitting spiritual aspirant for enlightenment and a participant in "hot yoga" stem from the same meditation lineage? Let's take a look at the basic concepts from which all these sprang.

Elëvën

Calm Abiding or Shamatha

A great number of the meditation practices and apps you come across fall into this group. It is the critical first step. The primary objective of Shamatha is to develop the mental discipline to quiet one's mind from all external and internal influences. It sounds simple, but as social beings, we are emotive, and as such, our thoughts, distractions, and internal dialogues are rife with emotion. These emotions act like epoxy glue, making it not only difficult to release the perpetual chatter in the mind but the emotional mindset or perception from which one views themselves and their world.

In Shamatha, the primary means of disrupting this process is to turn the mind's focus to one's breath. With the mind focused on each inhalation and exhalation, one becomes present in the moment. The simple conscious act of focusing one's breath dissipates scattered thoughts, allowing us to enter a calmer, clearer mind frame. In fact, focusing on one's breath, regardless of the activity is profoundly effective at bringing one into the body and the present moment, thereby strengthening the mind - body connection, facilitating harmony.

This reflects the traditional sitting meditation technique. The more formalized forms found within a spiritual framework prescribe specifics such as vows that are designed to aid in disciplining the mind and concentrating one's focus. Included among them are specifics regarding one's body posture during meditation, such as the sitting position, eye movement, etc. I will have something to say about this later.

This basic breath work meditation format has evolved in our modern world. Many of us have more sedentary working lives so the contemporary renditions and varieties of methods on offer are really wellness-focused practices. Old methods have had to adapt to our mentally over-stimulated world, thus incorporating body movements and breath work to facilitate the release of tension and stress. Yoga practices, Tai Chi, Qigong, martial arts, and dance (such as the Sufi Dervishes) are the older, more traditional forms of physical meditative practices that seek to bring discipline and balance between body and mind and spirit.

The solitary physical activity of walking is flexible and readily adaptive to developing a breathing practice that can aid in harmonizing the body and mind as well. The key to accomplishing the energetic harmony between the mind and body in any of these active forms will depend upon your mindful focus to actively clear the chaotic constant stream of thoughts from your mind.

Think of all those little timeouts you've given yourself when you "just needed a moment to clear your head and think for a second." Build on that! You already recognize and utilize this self-care technique! You know that with a quiet mind, one is open to listening. You know this practice works because you already use it! Performing in a restive part of your day will allow you to begin to listen to your body—to your internal energies. You're already off to a great start!

The body experiences everything! It doesn't matter whether it's a thought, an emotion, or from the physical realm. We are organisms of our environment. So it is absolutely critical that we find for ourselves a way to remove the agitation and the constant running scenarios that we indulge in without a thought! According to the principles of Shamatha meditation, a calm, quiet mind is the first step to healing the body. And, I have shown you that not only is this true but it is also true that a calm mind is only truly calm when the body is in homeostasis... with no internal agitated signaling.

We can also see that the initial dependency for care came from outside of ourselves, which created the habitual indulgence to always seek fulfillment and lay expectations on others and outside forces. With such an overwhelming preference for this outwardly directed activity, with little or no inward reflection, we only increase the seeking, grasping mental activities, which, in turn, increase our imbalances and end up triggering further emotional responses. A vicious circle, indeed.

So, we should adopt for ourselves a form of breathing practice. As you develop mindfulness and presence, especially if you incorporate healthy body movements, your body-mind energies will begin to balance and harmonize. When your mind and body coordinate harmoniously together, then the bodily ecosystem's natural resistance to stressors strengthens, allowing internal energies to flow more smoothly, thus healing the body and nervous system. It is a very natural, organic form of healing that is already within us. We only need to activate it.

Basically, once you have gained a quiet, still mind, then and only then... and I repeat, only then... do the body and mind reach a calm state—a form of homeostasis. In this calm, undisturbed state, the entire body's ecosystem experiences soothing.

As you build a little more breathing room and gain some measure of stability of mind, disruptive thoughts begin to fall away more easily, because you are not "entertaining" them and you will be happily surprised to observe that your body is beginning to respond as well. One reason folks know meditation is "good for you" is due in part to the "feel-good" factor to the body, not just the ability to relieve anxious thinking. It's a very healthy self-care activity that I strongly encourage.

This is the link between the spiritual aspirant and the "hot yoga" participant. Motivation and perspective. Their objectives may be different, but both are seeking that mind-body homeostasis: one focused through mental clarity and agility, the other through the expulsion of energies in the physical body and agility. Both will gain balancing benefits, but neither is truly a holistic approach without mindfully incorporating the other as well.

The spiritual aspirant needs body consciousness and exercise. The "hot yoga" participant needs mental agility and to develop mindfulness. Surprisingly enough, both need to gain better insight... and that requires a more in-depth understanding of the nature of their being to derive the balance between the "doing" and the "non-doing." It would seem that the spiritual aspirant has the advantage because of his commitment to dismantle himself to acquire this calm mind called "emptiness." Not so. But I might be getting ahead of you here, so let's hold that thought and walk through the second aspect of traditional meditation practice.

Twelve

Insight or Vipassana Meditation

Just in the same way that you begin to develop body-mind homeostasis in calm-abiding, so does the "trust" level of the body increase. Keep this in mind because it is important for us. I will speak more specifically to this point in the next section, but first I'll describe the basic Vipassana practice.

Vipassana meditation is really the second part of any true meditation practice—the other half of calm-abiding meditation, or Shamatha. The activity you perform within Insight or Vipassana meditation framework is only possible once you have acquired some stability in the body-mind homeostasis. During calm-abiding meditation, you are actively focusing your mind so that all those chaotic, anxious thoughts give way and are no longer distracting. You are no longer entertaining them. You are settling the ego down from constant stimulation. Giving it a big time-out moment.

In Vipassana, or insight meditation, however, you are actively engaged in the reflective process of looking at the harmful afflictions that trouble you, and you find understanding and peace with them. Insight meditation is advertised as the method to permanently eradicate afflictions via detailed techniques that focus upon identifying, analyzing, and applying the appropriate antidotes, eventually leading one to the "realization" that the afflictions are a whole lot of nothing, allowing us to "let it go"—to no longer grasp at it.

There are many religious, spiritual, and mediative disciplines in the world that have designed their specific methods of going through this mental process. Each has designed a version of insight meditation that is replete with its own unique terminology or way to guide and direct you through. Why? Well, this is the reflective side of meditation. You've created the "space" from calm-abiding, to allow you to look deeply into each affliction. So the mediation techniques offered are there to help you interpret your pain and to draw the "correct" conclusions. The goal, basically, will be to help direct your thoughts, how to understand the workings of the mind and guide you through the internal process of identifying your afflictions, ultimately, resolving them to be insubstantial... just the workings of the mind. This is where we got the "let it go" refrain. It's all a-whole-lot-of-nothingness recognized as the realization, thus allowing one to detach from the hurt, frustration, anger, etc.

If meditation has a bad connotation in your mind—beyond the time demands—then it's probably due to the confusion regarding all of these competing methodologies. Their stated objective and goal may be the same, but the fact that each touts a different version of accomplishing it is the confusing bit. How to differentiate?

Well... the difference, really, is only the proclivities of their respective religious or philosophical viewpoints, languages, and proscribed methods of disciplining your mind. How effective they are at guiding you to accomplishing this goal, is another matter. Since the methodologies are "mind-only" formulations and operate under the old paradigm, then the effectiveness of true mind-energy-body healing can be limiting. With some exceptions, of course.

Within Vipassana meditation, there is an "equalizing" component of the practice. It goes some way to ameliorating personal suffering by its "leveling" effect as one develops empathy and recognize the commonality of the suffering condition of all humanity. In tantra practices, this is called tonglen. Through tonglen, one performs the visualization of taking on the pain and suffering of others, internally transforming it, then sending out compassionate healing energy in return. There are many religious and spiritual ascetics who engage in this kind of meditative activity. Many consider this a spiritual practice of exercising compassion and for the purpose of developing empathy.

Although not recognized as such, tonglen, or equalizing, practice is a key component to healing, period. You and I have just completed this type of equalizing exercise through what we've just learned of our human nature from the previous pages. So, you see, you've got this! You now have this tool available to you.

Then there are healing forms of movement practices in Hatha yoga, Qigong and Tai Chi, that engage in connecting our energy with our bodies and with all of the universe. These movement practices provide subtle healing through toning, strengthening the bodies organs and tissues while opening internal pathways for energy, blood and oxygen to flow more smoothly.

This has been a rather broad look—just a sketch of the basic premise of the two aspects of traditional meditation practices. The specific mention of the equalizing and tonglen activities within Vipassana, if performed correctly, can be helpful for developing the mind-body connection. But the underlying principles and purpose of these two forms were not created specifically for direct healing, much less for healing wounds. They were designed to help you develop empathy and compassion, allowing you to see others as you do yourself. Infinitely valuable and necessary for building homeostasis, however, the goal of these practices is focused on adjusting your outward conduct so that you no longer contribute to your future suffering. Makes sense, doesn't it?

As I traversed through this part of the spiritual journey, I was discovering that aspects of the above practices were contained within the very meditation practices I created for myself as a child. As an empath, one becomes accustomed to the odd sensations of familiarity and knowing when there is no "rational" way in which one can explain how one knows without previous exposure. However, what it most clearly demonstrates is the commonality of our humanity. The methods codified by the gurus long ago and those of an attuned empathic child, speaks to the constancy of expression and human experience.

Yet, none of them described the core component of my practice that has proven to be a critical means of purification for my deep healing and transformation. It wasn't until I was completing the final edits for this book that I was introduced to an ancient purification practice that has a focus which closely resembles my own. I will mention the Chöd practice later in Chapter 24.

Alright. Let's assess where we are at the moment:

We know that focused breath work helps to center us and regain our presence—our compass.

We know that finding a suitable healthy, physical regiment incorporating breath work is a critical self-care practice that aids in bringing the mind-energy-body balance into a state of homeostasis. And we know that with the gained calmness of mind, we've given ourselves a space to communicate, and, for your mind—your ego—to listen to You!

Thë Budding Poët

With a violet eye
I see my view opens
up to what is:
presence.
the more I am awed
by the miracle of being,
the more present
and,
the longer I abide,
I aspire for my environment
to enjoy this bliss.
Thus, I look out
to extend healing,
through this gift to voice
a ray of light
through insight gleaned
over lifetimes traversed
to shine one's light
along the way is the heart
of this poet's song:
the poetry of a bodhisattva.

Thirteen

Meditation – Homeostasis

As stated at the very beginning, the effectiveness of any of our endeavors involves the correct perspective and motivation. So, any meditation practice one engages in has the potential to be effective. The opposite is true as well. From what point of view are you coloring your judgments? What is motivating you? The answers to these two questions are so vital to the effectiveness of anything and everything one does in life, be it meditation, employment, entertainment, sports, or sex. Fear is a huge unacknowledged motivating factor. The fear of avoidance, specifically, is one that has impeded us all.

One of the tasks of the book is to help alleviate the fear that comes with taking up a meditation practice. More bluntly, I wish to help remove the barriers that keep you from even trying.

A deep dive into our cosmic and evolutionary beginnings uncovered the overarching influence and impact that the attract/repel/bind calculus has on us, affecting our body's wellness and our mind's state of agitation, proving the root of all our emotional experiences and expressions. Recognizing that all humans share the same root causes—that none of it is truly You—will go a long way in mitigating your resistance... your fear of taking a closer look inside.

Recalibrating our view, if embraced and utilized during meditation, will be key to transforming your mind-energy-body healing exponentially. Of course, it takes time to break from the habits of a lifetime, of how we have understood and engaged in our world, so be gentle with yourself. It takes time. This will be your task... to grow accustomed to a more authentic reflection of You. You're remembering! We are confronting the old paradigm while it still operates in our world!

Now, I need to stop a moment here for an acknowledgment: We are now pivoting.

Although I have just outlined the traditional aspects of meditation, I've extracted the components valuable in a healing practice that incorporates both aspects of our true being: matter and energy; body and spirit; thoughts and emotions. We still need to practice viewing ourselves through the lens of non-duality, seeing how our energies play out much closer to home, in our day-to-day lives. What proceeds in the next section will require that I speak of things that are more deeply human, deeply intimate... at the bone of being.

You are on the verge of venturing into your own emotional world. You are a seeker. You are seeking a way to your Light—to that serenity and bliss. You are seeking self-love—to remember yourself. It takes courage to be vulnerable, especially with ourselves. Few venture down this path. The truth is, few do because of the fear of looking too closely at themselves.

You are the only proof needed to confirm this truth. We may feel discontented and troubled. We may feel inadequate. There is resistance, naturally. There is always an excuse. Too busy. Doing nothing feels selfish. You believe that diving into these dark waters, into the unknown, to perform this kind of internal work will only result in making you feel even worse about yourself. Right? Each and every one of us feels this. This is the depth of self-loathing... the lack of love we have for ourselves.

And, guess what? This "feeling" is the ego—the one that worked frantically to come up with schemes and notions that might "fix" or solve what you thought was "wrong." Well, this resistance is a defense mechanism of your ego trying to protect you from uncovering all those ugly bits. A desire to keep them masked and hidden so as not to reveal all your ego's errors in judgment. Who wants to admit they made a mistake? This is the old paradigm, though. It is this twisted sense of protection that keeps all that hurt front and center within you... and You off-center!

This inhibits you from becoming your authentic self. You know, the one you hide—the one deep within your heart that cries out within you, the one that you've stifled. Many of us have been so successful at sublimating our personal dreams and aspirations that we are no longer in touch with them. This is what I meant by being "off-center."

The resistance is a form of self-loathing... a denial of self-care, of loving compassion for You. But, in just these few pages, we've gained insight into the nature of our so-called ugly bits of faulty judgment and misunderstanding. We have unmasked the framework that all of our suffering is founded on to be wrong, so your so-called errors of judgment aren't truly yours to carry alone. We have all conducted ourselves thus, so there's really nothing to protect you from—nothing to hide from. It's a human thing, and we've exposed it.

The work to be done for you will be to bring you to a calm mind so that you can now engage in some clean-up work and get your internal communication channels flowing. It will allow you to break through all those energy blocks so your body can heal. Just remember, resistance is fear. It is sabotaging you and limiting you from living your life fully... happily on your terms.

Please, take a deep breath. Relax. You're doing fine. Return to your center, ground zero—to the truth.

We have traversed a great deal, and it will take time to absorb. Not because I've inundated you with concepts and terminology to memorize but rather because this pivoting into a new perspective is difficult. Yet, a releasing exercise that will slowly take root. This is the beginning of growth and opening up. Ultimately, it's about remembering. It's a liberating, unburdening, perspective that might feel uncomfortable for those who have been carrying a great deal of trauma, pain, and unhappiness inside them. That pain is real as long as it's inside of you. I love you enough to try to help you release it. I want you to love yourself enough to allow it.

I call to mind a Gordon Setter we adopted who had been neglected and kept in a small closed kennel for most of her life. Learning how to be free to walk and run and just be a dog took a great deal of love and patient support before she grew into the beautiful, graceful, happy dog that she truly was. She became a joy in our lives.

When one has been imprisoned and is suddenly allowed to go free, there is an entire reclamation process necessary. All that open space feels uncomfortable. Frightening. You feel exposed, naked. The not-so-funny irony is that it will feel like something is missing. Who are you except for all that stuff you held onto? All that you've experienced? How you've been treated? All that you believe you feel? That's who you are, right? Who are you if you were free of it all? Who would you want to be? How would you conduct yourself differently?

Part 3

Tantric Purification and Healing

Thë Trinity in All Things

How can this be?
What is this breath?
Great awareness. Great love.
Pure insight. Pure energy.
The great mother of all things conceived
within her nothingness, allowing
Her full potential expression.
Pure vision. Pure manifestation.
The whole of infinity within nothingness.
She conceived the perfect trinity
of all existence through great awareness.
Three energies, propensities to express
what might manifest.
Creating through opposing natures,
Ah, to merge, they balance.
Duality; the Mirror.
Neutral; equanimity.
Balance.
Friction of energies, frequency, dynamic oscillating
momentum and vibration occur.
Creating primary phenomena building
blocks of potential being:
sound, light, heat, density.
The interplay becomes the infinity
of all manifested matter that might become.
The divine source, omniscient awareness,
pure vision may have conceived
existence but only through great energy,
great love, desire for existence ...

for expression: for life ...
the becoming of all things from within itself;
opened the possibility of oxygen—
like a bellows, breath taken
within a conduit into electric energy.
Eons of time transpired to create precious human existence.
All sentient beings possess
the spark of life within,
divine consciousness seeking
expression through us, with us.

We are betwixt what is and what is not: divine consciousness.
Yet, we are the nothingness of her being;
we are the nothingness in all things;
we are the nothingness of being.

Fourtëën

Accëptïng Our Trüë Natürë

We have completed a look at our true being as part of the whole cosmology and the evolution that made us what we are: sentient beings with consciousness. Consciousness with the capabilities to actually comprehend our senses, recognizing and enhancing this precious existence by co-creating and manifesting what we can conceive of that will make us most happy during our time on this earth.

This beautiful earth, our home, offers to us all her bounty unconditionally. This state of being is only possible through the nature of Light—that clunky, simple calculus dictating that all within this realm is ever-transforming. The perimeters of this impermanence lie between birth and death. We, as human beings of matter and energy, become accountable for our well-being and that of our environment. It is a gift as long as we value it.

We are responsible for what we conceive and manifest into this paradise. We are responsible for the ecosystem of our world, our environment, our home, and ourselves. Planet Earth is no longer in balance. Collectively, we have only taken from her, exploited her. Just as we do of our bodies. We are not in harmony with our world because we have not cared for her or ourselves. Indigenous peoples have been trying to speak to this need. It is a voice crying for survival, for balance... for homeostasis. It is the voice of our children. It is a voice of true, holistic, compassionate self-love, and self-care for all of us. This voice arises from deep within us as beings of Light.

We are now turning to look closer to home, ourselves, and our society. It is how we have collectively shaped and created our world. I must draw your attention to examples that are uncomfortable. By looking at how the attract/repel/bind calculus and the resultant energies flow through our actions, emotions, and decisions in our day-to-day lives will help us to become more comfortable seeing in this new non-dual paradigm. Think of this as an initial purification phase built into your meditation practice. Recognition and acceptance will be the key to success here. Let us allow the emotional storms to wash over us. We will get wet, yes, but definitely refreshed once the clouds clear overhead. April showers, May flowers, right?

You can feel the cold winds but you can't see them until you attempt to resist them.

There is no way around this truth—your puddle. We've all got one! This reflects the tension, the disconnect, and the disparity between the two aspects of our being: energy and matter. This disparity is the suffering, poor health conditions, poverty, and general unhappiness playing out in our lives. We've already talked about the conditions under which all becomes... that simple bit of calculus that rules all of duality. So, as the Buddhists say, let's make mud!

Remember, we are humans, and humans make mistakes. This is what we are hurting from, right? So, let's take a fresh look so we can recognize and acknowledge as much. By accepting our dirt and these emotional storms, we'll free them, and from this mud, you'll begin to bloom like the Light in the Lotus... as your truer self. Oops! I keep getting ahead of you. I'm just so excited for You!

By doing so, we aren't just naming the monster, but we are accepting ourselves. Our fallibility. Hey! We've already punished ourselves and one another, so let us free ourselves! Please. Let's name it and release it! Let's release what no longer serves our health or well-being. Doing so will actually change your world too. The benefit to going through this together will be the gained experience, which will trigger memories and hopefully a small measure of comfort as you begin to view life in a more organic, non-dual, holistic manner.

I will be presenting, for your consideration, a few examples to demonstrate some of our choices and assumptions about how we act out in this life of ours through the paradigm of the dualism of fear. There is no conflict or imbalance when we are in homeostasis, content and happy. So, it is to those choices from imbalance, from fear that we must turn our eyes.

What the mind can conceive is limitless; therefore, it would be impossible for me to discuss all the ramifications resulting from fear. Each of us experiences fear daily—along with the havoc they wreak.

And, because reality is non-dual, so too will I focus on the flow and movement of our energies in hopes of showing you how to look at our societal and personal choices in the same manner to see how our thoughts and energies create emotional weather patterns that are as observable as the local new station's doppler map.

So, we need to look at fear, anger, worthiness, depression... and gender and self-identity while we're at it. You know: the biggies—that which we've chosen to rule our lives to date. Yeah, the old paradigm. All of these factors are interconnected and of the same energy... the shadow, dark side of Light. As you'll see, it will be difficult to determine where to pin a flag claiming one section as fear and one as anger. So, the use of the aforementioned headers will only be conditional. The objective here is to give you a few beginning avenues that might resonate and provide you a means to engage and navigate these kinds of issues when they arise for you personally.

Breathe. Remember, on the other side is the authentic You. The one you will joyously embrace.

Okay, take a deep breath, and let's go...

Fifteen

Fear – Seeds of Anger

One of the most horrifying and damaging errors we make when we're trying to sort out and understand something that has gone wrong in our lives is the constant internal reenactment. To play out whatever grievance, anger, trauma over and over in our heads. We always think we are trying to understand what and how the hurt happened to us or we are trying to get our "facts" straight so we can correct or demand validation, justice, and fairness. The horror is that our bodies, as biological organisms, experience no distinction between memory and reality. The body experiences everything you feed it, regardless! You are creating that pain—all that harmful energy within yourself—over and over again.

Every time you relive an event, you create it through your energy, your passion. In turn, your mind-ego generates an emotional association, and from this, it's experienced within the body. You chose to experience the event in your mind, body, and spirit over and over and over again as well. When it's a positive nurturing experience, this is good. However, most of the time, we are focused on the stuff that confuses us, hurts us, worries us, pisses us off, and frustrates us.

This mental agitation builds up over time. Remember, the ego's work is constantly seeking out and taking in stimuli and interpreting. Constantly! Even our dreaming reflects this. The body experiences the pain and trauma over and over and over. You are attacking yourself over and over and over again. You can clearly see that this will damage your health and well-being from the inside out. It's truly gut-rendering.

It's of paramount importance that you keep yourself tethered to your purpose. To calm the agitation is the primary aim of calm-abiding meditation.

It's why we took time early on to place ourselves at our centers of what and who we are—at the calm before emotions created the storm of pain and suffering. This is another key reason why it's so critical to have the right perspective and motivation secured and at the ready. It's also why it's so important to wait until you have gained some stability of mind such that you are able to disrupt your thoughts and halt any triggering emotional pulls you've associated with them. Otherwise, you end up in that never-ending emotional whirlpool of reenactment, which ensures self-loathing, magnifying and intensifying emotional turmoil... punishing yourself as a repeat offender! Very heavy energy, indeed.

So, this is basically a heads-up—a warning to take it slow. You are here to discover the real you and shed much of the stuff that has been revealed to you as not really You after all. So don't cause yourself further harm by constantly rehashing the minutiae. Stop punishing yourself! Hold your head high. Focus on observing the energy within you and surrounding you in those events, in the emotions, and in your thoughts about them. It's your trail... so, follow the energy. What kind of energy was projected and utilized in the incident? What energy did you use? This is your trail out of the tears that will help you understand the truth behind the pain. This leads to self-discovery.

There are many manifestations of fear whirling within us and generated by us out in the world. The fear of others, illness, poverty, death, ugliness, loneliness, spiders, violence, and the unknown. External conditions and appearances dominate when our focus is outwardly seeking. When our expectations aren't met or the outside world presents us with the unfamiliar, we are understandably confused. Confusion and frustration are ignorance wrapped in fear.

Our internal attract/repel/bind calculus sets off the withdrawing, the inward pulling, and the repel energy. We actually end up drawing to us exactly what we fear! We become fearful. Our world becomes a fearful place.

Sixtëën

Fëar – Thë Angër of Povërty

There is this mistaken truth in economics that we have all accepted as the way things are in this world. It is this notion that in this world there is only a finite abundance to be had. It is, then incumbent upon us to do all we can to obtain for ourselves our "fair share" of that "piece of the pie." The harm and devastation of this mentality are beyond words. It appears to drive the entire human enterprise of existence here on earth. And, if you don't, fail or succeed, you will be consumed by it.

The intense need to amass great "wealth," constricting resources, innovation, and prosperity... not to mention, food, healthcare, and the like for so many among us. This reflects fear. It is the drawing inward, greedy, needy, pulling energy of the repel energy, ironically. These outwardly directed activities that can look like aggression actually mask the repel, drawing inward activity of fear. This is the force that rationalizes militarization, wars, tariffs, strip mining, economic policies, ecological resources, palatial homes, gated communities, national borders, and land ownership.

I already spoke earlier of the unconditional nature of our planet's bounty, yet our unbalanced demands and greed have adversely affected the homeostasis of the Earth. There is plenty to meet all our needs and wants … just not our greed.

The power of this energy in this world is so aggressive and destructive, and its energies are expended through war and sexual violence. This is self-generating—self-actualizing. It is chosen by us. But it is not true. It is only true because we make it so... allowing it to be so. Feed it, engage in it, let it occupy your thoughts and concerns, then it influences your perspective, affects your motivations: well, then it becomes true enough. But it is still only real if you wish it to remain so.

We have built our world this way, but none of it is actually real or true. We can remember to choose a different paradigm.

Sёvёntёёn

Fёar – Angёr of Worthlёssnёss

Greed is both fear and anger. Fear of poverty can produce the kind of aggressive, outwardly-directed energy that we can readily observe in the extremes of capitalism, Ponzi schemes, tax-dodging, theft, and vandalism, to name just a few. In our personal lives, we've been taught to seed our prosperity by dressing for success and the fake-it-till-you-make-it philosophy widely advertised in the corporate world. Think of the stereotypical sales executive, realtor, or investment banker we've come across who drives leased luxury cars dressed to the nines. Even religious and spiritual leaders have succumbed to this show of wealth... all to reflect the financial success they desire and want you to invest or believe in.

Every couple of years, another motivational speaker reemerges on the corporate circuit to convince you that such shows of wealth reflect your worthiness, your power, and your success in the world. You deserve it. If you don't have it, you didn't want it enough or you didn't deserve it. It's a pseudo-religion of capitalism. This outward show only sets up a further fear of failure, driving more aggressive behavior... or its inverse, the imploding depression of internalized anger. This is aggression and fear in plain sight: the extremes of its deprivation... such as homelessness. All self-generating and self-actualizing. This reflects us.

We are well-intentioned humans who wish to be happy and prosperous yet fail to see that this engagement toward our employment and our contributions to the world is through a paradigm of fear.

Then there is our predilection to time. We see it as linear. We created pie charts to encompass the whole of things but we graph all things in linear time to reflect progress. Profit. Enhancement. We ignore the circle of life. We ignore the signs of our seasons. We ignore the fragility of our unknowable lifespan. We don't keep our "expectations" within the cycle of things or in balance with our home, Mother Earth. This forgetting—this misunderstanding—is why we become greedier all the time. We were so clever to comprehend and conceive time, but in the dualistic world, this human family prefers to see and experience time as linear. Very unfortunate.

Of course, we need prosperity, security, and the like, but this must be accomplished by fully manifesting the gifts and talents that contribute to our well-being and that of the world. Not recognizing or developing our talents means that we are deprived of the very gifts that are the source of our personal happiness and our means of livelihood, of manifesting them as our contribution to the benefit of our societies where they will enrich the lives of those in our community, our world. So, in truth, our undeveloped, un-manifested gifts and talents intensify the deprivation in our world, adding to the further degradation and poverty of resources for the human family and our planet. We are all harmed, and we all suffer from it. These gifts and talents—the "who" you truly are—the You that was meant to thrive in this blessed life.

We need a world that embraces our authentic development. Each of us is endowed with gifts and talents to develop and manifest... to fulfill our purpose, our belonging, for the benefit of our happiness and our world.

You do this from the heart, from compassion, not from fear. And, definitely not simply for its monetary gain. Money is not wealth.

Eighteen

Fear – Entertaining Our Anger

Look at our society's preferred forms of film entertainment. We actually seek out violence and horror with an occasional romantic comedy thrown into the mix. Our predilection for extreme and intense emotional experiences reflects our conditioning. It also points out our mistaken "need" for such intense expressions to "confirm" and get "in touch" with ourselves.

Who are you, but what you are able to feel, express, or do? Right? Do you actually believe this?

We are in a world where the actual "doing life" is more often confined to an office cubicle and computers.

There are fewer and fewer of us engaged in the types of physical activities of work that older generations did. Our service industry, the foundational work supporting our basic care—be it healthcare, education, feeding, clothing, or housing—is now crowded out with the likes of legal, insurance, protective, and information services. Non-physical and highly stressful.

Less engagement with our bodies and our environment is not conducive to retaining healthful, balanced bodies. Without adequate, healthy physical activity, the imbalances end up resurfacing in other activities and forms... the need to express outwardly in all manner of forms. They resonate within us, but are our forms of employment and entertainment truly cathartic, meaningful, and healing? Or, do they resonate because they reinforce some unexpressed emotive, congested energies within us? Are you, in fact, indulging in reenactment and adding harmful energies onto already existing wounds?

We have removed calisthenics and physical education from our schools. We've removed music, the arts, drama... all means of healthy bodies, healthy minds, healthy spirits. Why did we make these choices for our children? Why do we short-change our future in this way? Or, by excluding or tailoring information that will blind us from making healthy, informed decisions? But, we feed our children with violence and blue light, destroying their eyes. Is it any wonder why our schools are now dangerous places where armed guards and guns are now a feature of the curriculum? Where our children now kill one another? Is this love?

The pandemic has highlighted how little we value our own self-care or those that labor to provide it. Who has been most harmed ... especially those who lost their lives... yes, the very souls of the service industry who carried us on their backs through this pandemic. All those who provide our basic human services, the mothers, our health-care workers, our grocers, caregivers, teachers, artists, services, farmers, and all those who labor to feed us. Our own survival and care systematically revealed to not have been a priority for us. Inadequate pay and conditions along with the lack of healthcare and transportation at the societal level reveals how little we prioritize the well-being of our human family. Why? This is not love.

Road rage is impatient anger linked to an agitated mental state. It is easily recognizable as fulfilling the bodily need to push out and release the stagnating, built-up tension, and agitated energy that was contained inside. A storm waiting to happen. A very inappropriate means of attempting to reach internal balance—homeostasis—wouldn't you agree? That road rage began long ago and has deep roots in fear that turned to anger; it was not an isolated incident. Any one of us can recall many incidences in our lives where we lashed out or found ourselves overly upset about a minor concern, not fully understanding the force of our actions. Here it is.

If and when you suffer moments of impatience, let the circumstances speak to you. Let it be a call to help return you to calmness. The situation may, in fact, have occurred at just the moment you most needed reflection. The universe does work with us. You would be shocked by how much of that built-up, yucky, agitated energy you will burn off just by allowing circumstances to help create the time and space for yourself. Even more shocking will be the discoveries that you can make in that "space" you allow into your being-ness during these occurrences. I will interject a personal note to clarify that when I say "burn off," I also mean burn calories, because I've been amazed at the improved strength and curve of my core, my abdomen, over these couple of years of practice. If you are calmer, you are less likely to stress-eat a full bag of family-sized chips or nosedive into that tub of ice-cream. That's a real diet plan that is for keeps, and you don't have to count calories.

Similar is the release of ardent sports fans, who end up in altercations... or just yelling at their television sets. They are drawing upon those deeply rooted constricted, agitated tensions within. Many would defend themselves, saying that they're exhausted from very stressful workweeks and that this entertainment is a harmless, socially acceptable means of release. Maybe, maybe not.

How enjoyable is it truly to engage in an activity that infuriates you and raises your blood pressure? That pisses you off? Just asking? I mean, if you want to do something that infuriates you, learn how to play a musical instrument! Honestly, there are more beautiful ways of being!

This energy you create within yourself is your power source. You can engage in any endeavor. Manifest your dreams! Try things. Discover hobbies. Create art, make music, grow a garden. This energy is your wellspring from which we build the world. Enhance life. Open yourself.

With mindfulness, this open energy allows for breakthrough communications that inspire collaboration or give us the drive to rescue someone from a burning building or to simply be willing to put our foot on the brake, slow down, merge into the flow of traffic at its own speed, and use the gained time to practice breath work.

This can be a life-saving, valuable expenditure of one's energies! Remember, I told you I would return to the image of the two equally opposing energies? Their power is their balanced charge. Neither attract nor repel. Ground. Return to yourself. Slow to the flow of the traffic and bring that slower pace within you. This is the best way you can ensure that you will reach your destination... and in life.

We claim to be health-conscious these days and self-aware, so we already know how to expend that pent up energy. Incorporate healthy physical activity: jogging, tennis, deep-sea diving, or maybe cleaning out gutters, building a playground in the neighborhood, or gardening, or just take a good long walk to have a good think. We depend upon our modern health care to fix whatever harm we cause our bodies, but remember: medicine is an intervention; it rarely heals. We heal ourselves.

Why give away your power and become part of the "way things are" at all? Why not empower yourself?

If we are what we do, express, and feel, then why do we choose combative, aggressive forms of release? Do they actually help? Are they truly constructive and healing? Are we being mindful? The competitive spirit and drive exhibited informs us that this combative energy is suspect. It comes from that sense of "them vs us," of winners and losers... of aggression. This kind of release is actually not a healthy, transformative release but an expression of the same aggressive energy pushing outwardly.

Nineteen

Fear – Small Indulgences

There are so many other forms of subtle daily assaults we engage in that reflect fear and aggression toward ourselves that hide within our entertainment outlets. Eating disorders, obesity, unhealthy food options and/or choices, binge-eating, alcohol, and drug abuse. None of it supports healthy, loving, self-care. All of these things stem from a sense of lacking, deprivation, fear, or maybe even worthlessness. Constant eating to mask and cover up or to seek comfort. Not eating on the other hand is a corrosive self-loathing fear, a desire to escape from one's own being-ness. All of them reflect misguided responses to fulfill an internal "need" or imbalance—that of affection and care. These are self-sabotaging behaviors.

Gossip is a toxic corrosive form of fear. This fear builds divisiveness that often turns aggressive. It has been rebranded in the workplace as an opportunity for intel-gathering. Gossip is never needed to acquire honest, reliable information. Period. We believe we are empowering ourselves with knowledge of hidden agendas and motivations for our own betterment and affording ourselves the opportunity to seed our own views to direct the discourse. Invariably, as we have all become victims of gossip, we gain some insight into its ugly side as a means to validate insecurities and a vehicle to exercise one's own emotional release of venom.

Gossip builds on distrust—the paradigm of "them vs us." It is a rather unfortunate sign of self-loathing. Not trusting oneself is a form of insecurity. Not trusting yourself causes you to not trust the environment or those you interact with. When you aren't centered in yourself, you don't know yourself and this fact plays in equal proportion outwardly as distrust. Of course, believing that this distrust is really "out there in the world" and then behaving from this perspective will only bring about the very results that we feared. Another vicious circle.

Our social-networking etiquette (or lack thereof) bullying, gaming … all forms of outwardly directed expenditures of negative energetic release... of attacking outwardly. Violence. Many believe it reflects how "woke" they are. We are feeding violence unto ourselves. Yet, another form of entertainment that we indulge in and actually "enjoy"... all for the "release" it provides us—temporarily.

Of course, this form of negative energy, which plays out in the smallness of our personal lives and our workplaces, also drives similar endeavors on larger-scale societal activities that draw like-minded individuals together into divisiveness, conflict, and violence, invariably building an "us-vs-them" paradigm. Our major religions and institutions reflect this … for they are human constructs. The healthiest forms bring about a collective voice for discourse and change for the betterment of our societies as a whole, but when their agendas are dwarfed, frustrated, or their voice is perceived as a threat, they can become the means of civil unrest, violence, great upheaval.

Truë Compassion

I am the most precious of Beings:
the light within
the rainbow reflecting
off your tear—
Dharmadhatu's wisdom form
the hearer of cries,
manifesting spontaneous
compassion—
arising from that
intimate embrace of complete surrender,
deep acceptance, and love for all.

Love Heals All

Twenty

Fear – Corrosive Expectations

We are currently observing segments of our human family that are fearful and uncertain of the huge changes occurring in our world. They are resisting through irrational, unhealthy choices, such as risking their own health and that of their communities by refusing to vaccinate. Each of these individuals bears the smallpox scar on their arms as beneficiaries of the thing that they now fear. There have been years of unresolved fear, confusion, frustration, and anger building from within their personal lives. So, the opportunity to collectively come together and focus on a simple health issue as the catalyst to expend all that congested, agitated energy feels "right" and "justified."

It feels right because there is now an object at which to direct all that unspent energy, thereby gaining some semblance of "release"—some relief, from all that agitated corrosive energy within themselves. This only draws others who hold similar grievances of resentment and bitterness within them, who, too, seek redress. This aggressiveness, when exerted, inhibiting or impeding change on our societal level feels like power. For some of our kinsmen, this short-term blocking feels effective and empowering where it has been missing from the more meaningful areas of their personal lives. This power is most deceptive and volatile... and temporary.

The inverse, deeply hidden, and most corrosive forms of fear's anger is what we most ardently protect—even from ourselves. Buried expectations that were never fulfilled, which led to resentment, bitterness, jealousy, and envy. This results in mistrust and can act out in ways like the examples of spiteful gossip, eating disorders, and anti-vax sentiments previously mentioned. The same corrosive fears that beget aggression permeate racial discrimination... or any form of discrimination against what is unknown, not understood.

Many of our institutionalized religious belief systems reflect a horrifying display of fear and self-loathing. The desire to be a stabilizing, guiding influence for our highest aspirations and principles of ethics and benevolence, have, in fact, made them static, resistant, constraining forces less able to serve the healing of body and spirit.

From my non-dual eye, I recognize the male fear and self-loathing in our religions. To seek to know all things, have an answer for all things, and possess all things is a sign to seek to control all things, which only gives rise to discrimination, judgment, and punishment.

As such, one becomes a toxic force, corrupting the very principles one professes to uphold. To be imperfect, sinful beings where we are to sacrifice love, beauty, music, dance, joy, health, happiness, as a penance for being human... because we are not gods, I suppose. We have so misunderstood! The attract/repel/bind calculus is easy to observe here. All of this results from not knowing how to love ourselves, thus not being able to love one another. The efforts to help guide us to our higher, better selves have also led to some of the most horrific instances of discrimination, divisiveness, and violence in our human history.

Well-intended, like-minded souls develop a framework to explain and understand their world, seeking succor from the confusion and unknowable forces in the world. All of the world's major religions have been hijacked from true spiritual guidance to justify power through wealth-amassing schemes, the justification of violence against others... and most vehemently against women as the cause of human weakness—the source of all desires and the degradation of our innate power to become like the divine.

We can see these energies playing in and out in our lives, in our society and in our personal lives. These forces flow in and out of all the others, interconnected, interdependent. There truly is no independence in anything we conceive. There is no act we engage in that is truly independent. We choose and share values of one sort or another, collectively, to support these values within the society at large. This opens the door to the aforementioned attract-repel-bind aspects of the calculus playing out on the microscopic, through every level our lives to the macro, cosmic scale. This is the climate of our energetic weather—the weather we create for ourselves from not knowing ourselves... not remembering ourselves. We choose what weather pattern we wish to associate with.

As you can see, all the weather patterns of our agitated thoughts and emotions flow inter-connectedly. In the Light, you flower like a beautiful mandala—a lotus—but these hot, agitated flames we've generated within us hide the fact that we are crying for healing waters.

There really is no need for us to concern ourselves with the motives or faults of anyone else. They are just as confused and lost. So, recognize all your suffering is inter-connected. Begin to observe how your energies act and react. Watch and feel your emotions. Where are they flowing? For what purpose? As our above view revealed, all manifesting forms of emotion that flow from fear become versions of anger, worthiness, depression, bitterness, resentment, jealousy, envy, and the like.

None of this is healthy, yet it flows out of us into our society—our world—in all the varied permutations that we humans can conceive of. Seemingly all to mask our underlying fear of not knowing who we are—or the nature of our environment. A truly twisted attempt to sooth ourselves, wouldn't you say? Throughout your life and the whole of human history, have you ever heard of or witnessed any of these uses of fear to have truly soothed us or been of the benefit of others? Mindless, harmful forms of self-care, indeed.

This brings us to gender and identity. A most divisive, volatile, and vast topic, but it gets at the heart of this dualistic world we live in and who and what we are. This realm of dualism rules supreme and is held up as the underpinning for most of our faulty views of ourselves and our world. Recognizing this truth will test your skill at viewing life from a more non-dual perspective.

Twenty One

Fear – Gender – Our Identity

So, we've taken a horrifying glimpse of the world we created with our dependency and internal tension. We built our world with this dominant perspective. Channeling what we do in the world through fear and anger is like infecting every aspect of our lives. It is the dominant energy driving mankind at the moment, and it affects us more substantially, more unknowingly, than we are comfortable admitting. Even our well-intended efforts fail to fully satiate us when we start from that faulty perspective of the old paradigm. We are increasingly unable to know that there is any other way of being or responding in the world. We forget ourselves.

We have been blinded by our own Light, unaware of our energies and the true source of our emotional nature. That blindness led to our over-reliance on and investment in the outward conditions and appearances of this realm of dualism. The old paradigm of dualism holds such sway over the affairs of humans for one primary reason: sexuality, our gender, our identity, and who we are allowed to become, determined by the physical body we inhabit.

Dualism is such an overpowering influence. Sexuality is used as the fundamental essence of its truth. I'm sure you'll have a flood of examples that come to mind unbidden. Dualism between the two sexes, encoding discrimination in our religions, laws, and homes. Something is unhealthy and imbalanced in our human family. Is there something behind all this that we don't find in high school physiology textbooks?

Generally speaking, our physical bodies develop into either male or female forms. However, you are both matter and spirit; physical and energy. You are of a non-dual nature housed within a dualistic form so that you can inhabit and experience this life. Your higher being and your energy/spirit nature are non-dual. As such, like the Light of our divine nature, there are no distinctions, no barriers of being-ness, and no inhibitions about developing and flourishing with the wholesome talents that desire to be expressed through the body it inhabits ... regardless of the physical form one might inhabit: male, female, or otherwise.

The energy you derive through each breath you take is a precious, charged source of energy that your body uses to operate the entirety of the human body's enterprises—be it the heart, itchy toe, or thyroid—just as readily as it allows you to utilize this energy to generate your thoughts, your emotions, your dreams, your perceptions and to then provide you the very drive and energy to physically manifest them.

You are a powerhouse! But not because you are male. You are an alluring delight to behold! But not because you are female. Your true nature is not troubled by sexuality. Your energetic being wants to express and create; it doesn't matter what physical form it resides within.

You resonate with others through the synergy of your emotive natures. In non-dual awareness, you will recognize what energies connect you to those around you, allowing for meaningful connections and relationships. With little or no awareness, our dualistic selves channel these energy expressions as sexual attraction, passion, excitement, hate, etc. So limiting, such a pity. We determine how we will channel and ultimately utilize the energy within us. Yet, we have been blind to our true nature. Our being as Light is a dynamic force. This is our agency. This is what it is to be fully human. Energy body. Physical body. Let us embrace ourselves. Being born female or male is not what inhibits us.

In this dualistic world, we have an idiom: misery loves company: this is just so. We draw the energies of our core to us like moths to the flame. So the paradigm of viewing your existence through duality is a prison... not the prism of your Light body. We have been very short-sighted, and we have suffered horribly for not embracing our true non-dual natures.

One of the bizarre realizations that arise with the non-dual view is to see that we humans have almost understood things— almost conceived things rightly—yet somehow gotten it wrong. Any deviation from the center casts a long shadow. If we start with the wrong understanding, all that we conceive will be flawed, no matter how brilliant. Such as this unfortunate example of having gotten things backward: this maleness thing about physical power and shows of strength, force, and ambition as admirable traits of leadership. We have this belief that we are these physical bodies with rational minds that make independent decisions for our best interest. We mistakenly believe we are acting out forcefully in the world, using the enhancing energy of the Yang, the masculine, the positively charged energy in this existence of duality. In fact, shows of force are sure signs of weakness—of imbalance.

All that he-man stuff proves to be of the negative, drawing in/repelling energy grounded in fear. Our old paradigm that institutionalized the male as the positive, protective, generating force in this dualistic realm proves to be highly suspect in the Light of the non-dual view. Even by way of the descriptions used in the old paradigm, the expenditure of all this "masculine" energy is actually what is collectively recognized as the receptive, weak, negative "female" energy. Is there not a grand paradox here? Do you see the problem? A definite blind spot!

We are Light beings of non-duality. We are physical bodies of duality. When you bring your body and spirit in balance; you empower yourself.

Part 4

Active Healing Meditation

Truë Compassion

It seemed such a simple matter
when embarking upon this venture—
All this nothingness to ask a simple question:
Who am I?
That Which IS
... became ...
... from the aeons of becoming,
having recognized the self
in the cosmos of light and space,
opening, ever receptive, to allow
ever-flowing definitions—
manifesting planets,
stars, suns, and moons
to a rare jewel, indeed,
that came from the heart wisdom—
the mother of all things:
a paradise, a garden, a nirvana ...
possessing lush abundance—
where the inorganic became
organic breathing beings.

"Ah, I am this! Such delight!
What more might become?"

And this becoming self, ever receptive,
opened to allow all things that might,
to become ...
... Ah, now is the time of the human;
evolving at the border between
what is and what is not...
their holy aspirants labor to deconstruct
their self-made identities
while I rush forward to fill their hearts.
"Take courage, dear ones, ask!
I will tell you of your true nature."

"This venture, embarked upon,
the ending becoming the beginning ...
"Oh, joy, you are of my nature!
We define one another!"
All this busyness is nothing more;
nothing less. It is nothing.
Let it be."

Twënty Two

Hëaling from thë Insidë Out

It is clear that we over-identify ourselves in the physical form. We clearly recognize all the energies and emotions we use as sentient beings, yet we are having a difficult time recognizing that all "that" energy exerted from you encompasses your energy body... your power source. Think of night-vision glasses. They see your heat, a low-frequency visualization of your energy body.

It's time to accept our divine non-dual energy bodies. It's time to bring about the homeostasis of our true natures of body and spirit—matter and energy. It's time to remember who we truly are and become fully empowered humans.

I hope this active form of tonglen equalizing and of Chöd purification opened you to seeing and recognizing how critical it is for us to shed all this darkness from our Light. It is time to transform our darkness into color. When you shine your Light, it will not only shed the darkness from your heart but it will dispel the darkness around you, benefiting others. As we each begin to reflect more of the Light of our true selves and the darkness falls away, we will also become calmer, less aggressive, less agitated.

By showing examples of how these energies act out through us into the world as well as internally, I hope you will begin to recognize them for yourself. Not to judge, no. Once you begin to observe the energies that flow in and out of your day-to-day life, you will experience the truth of it. This will, in turn, help you to observe this energy within your own conduct! Within your own body. This type of visualization technique is simple and requires no imagination because you will begin to remember yourself... and love yourself.

Once you begin to see in this way more readily, your emotions become less engaged. You are observing, giving yourself that "space" to understand more holistically and respond from your center. This pivoting in your thinking is to be celebrated. It is your power. Your meditation practice will only strengthen this, freeing you further. Thus, the work in meditation transforms into a true form of relief and release... a healing exercise.

Once you begin to "feel" the relief from your meditations in this way, you will be recovering your inherent power to choose. This is very empowering. This is truly the pivoting of perspective in action. You begin to empower yourself to decide to respond differently, to engage in activities differently and for reasons that are more authentically reflective of what you desire... and of who you really are. True self-care.

When you can separate out the emotions from the energies and the situation or person(s), then the storm begins to slowly subside and clear. It is this release that frees you from the emotional attachment so you can begin to discern what was truly at the heart of what troubled you. You will, thus, begin to make healthier choices.

This will allow the magic to truly begin...

When I say "magic," I am attempting to evoke that energetic charge that you will begin to experience, which feels something like "delight." The gurus of meditation call this "bliss." It's your internal Light coming through. It's an experience of your body and spirit in homeostasis... and it's an affirmation, a positive expression that feeds the heart and soul—most definitely healing for the body. I want this for you!

I will specifically mention a very powerful tool I recommend that has come down to us from ancient practices: mantras and chants. A most sacred form of meditative practice that can be quite powerful. They are designed so that the recitations of mantras of specific sounds and tones in a specific pattern will resonate and harmonize with the internal energies of the body... all through the use of emptiness (air/breath) to promote specific types of healing and agility within. It is active body work. It is a high form of spiritual work...

We have been so out of touch with our bodies and our energies, it is critical that we begin by bring more physical activity and breath work into our lives, consistently, as this will help us to offset the overstimulation and agitation of our minds and emotions.

Incorporating movement with breath work is quite healing and active—tantric. We humans have recognized this power of breath, chanting, and bodywork: utilizing it even collectively in such undertakings as the performance of some great physical feat of labor or congregating in cathedrals for prayer.

Mantras are widely adaptive and are used today by gurus, therapists, motivational coaches, school counselors, and the like. Utilizing personal affirmations, chant and mantras is a targeted means of disrupting negative thought patterns that you may be locked into due to the emotional energy that has ensnared you. You know, it's the epoxy glue that binds those thoughts and your internal energies together, wreaking havoc. In the beginning, you will have a great deal of the daily stresses and anxieties to extinguish before you can even get to a calm-abiding practice, so using mantras will be of tremendous help.

Standing in the middle of your living room singing and dancing as wildly as can be is a wonderful way of shaking off the day's excess anxieties. Or a game of tag with the kids. Be sure to laugh. Laughing at ourselves is healing to body and spirit. Divine play! So much healthier than yelling at your television set, wouldn't you agree?

All of us have a playlist of tunes that evoke all kinds of emotions in us. You are engaging your emotive energy. And, you are using your favorite songs as a form of mantras. What messages are you reinforcing in yourself? Look at the content of your playlist. You will discover that you might be feeding yourself negative, self-sabotaging energy... keeping it at your center... putting You off-center. As you progress in your meditations, you will naturally grow out of certain kinds of messaging and start to replace them with music that better resonates with your new state of being.

You may have noticed by now that I'm only pointing out activities you already engage in during your daily life as a means for meditation... of mindfulness. You have all the means at your disposal. Truthfully, your daily life is your spiritual life. Let me repeat: There is no separation between your spiritual life and your daily life! What you do in your day to day live is what builds your heaven, fulfilling those dreams that were meant for you. Your life is not meant to be a daily grind... each day, each activity we engage in, communicates. Your day is to take delight in. We are beings of light and form—spirit and body, matter and energy. We only need to return to our centers, embracing and harmonizing with our true natures.

Habituating your practice means prioritizing manifesting love in your life. Your daily life is your spiritual life.

The true result of meditation is learning to love oneself, not to discipline oneself. For this reason, I take issue with the instructions regarding holding one's body in an exacting manner, with eyes half-open, etc. It is something akin to the disciplinary mode of fake-it-till-you-make-it kind of instruction. However, recognize that all that twitching, fidgeting, skin tingling, body movement... is energy being expressed through your body. It is releasing. It should be allowed. You should be mindful of its activity and where it is in your body. Make it part of your practice while you need to. The more you incorporate physical movement in your day and just before sitting on your cushion, the less of this activity you will undergo. They are signs of the agitated energies and blocks within you. This is where a simple 5 Elements qigong practice is especially beneficial. As you progress, this activity dissipates, reflecting signs that your energies, your emotions, and your body are coming together towards homeostasis. You will find that as you progress, your body will naturally find its center in that prescribed sitting pose conducive to true physical alignment for clearing and balancing your energies. Let the body speak. Learn to listen to it.

I have tried to show you how adaptive and flexible I believe this directive to be. Utilize activities or substitute activities you are already engaged in that will help you create "space" for yourself. You can turn off the television. There is a great amount of time and space to be gained by disengaging from digital forms of entertainment. If you commute to and from work, use that space for some breath work and centering. If your meditation practice begins with naps, so be it. Your body needs it. If you begin your journey with your playlist, that is wonderful. You'll begin to recognize what you are telling yourself about You. This will be quite revealing!

There is no need to reinvent the wheel, so to speak. You need to engage in self-care activities that incorporate the body and your energies so that you can build awareness and become more receptive to listening to your inner needs and aspirations. Reflexology, yoga, massage, breath work, Qigong, Tai Chi, sound therapy, singing, mantras, walking, dance, and acupuncture are just a few readily available forms to consider. Naturopathic, Ayurveda, and Chinese medicine are holistic disciplines that strive to bring better alignment to one's mental, physical, and spiritual self. Acupuncture and reflexology are specific forms designed to move and clear energy within your body while providing pain relief.

Many forms of physical activity can be worthy contenders for dissipating excess built-up energies. However, competitive sports are not conducive to our purpose, so I would not recommend them as forms of physical activity for attuning and calming your internal energies with the body. For those of us who are susceptible to depression or low energy, physical activity is the perfect prescription to help you build internal energy and stamina. If you have limited mobility, the challenge might be greater, but any efforts you make will prove beneficial.

As for the eyes? As any practitioner of Taoism or Chinese medicine knows, we lose most of our Qi, vital life force energy, out of our eyes. And, in today's modern world, visual stimulation dominates. The purpose for teaching the half-open method was originally meant to be administered only to boys and men, who may need it as a means to deplete excess energies... and a way for the lamas or gurus to assess the student's wakefulness and mindfulness during meditation training. Women were never to do so. Women, I recommend that you close your eyes. I would also make the same recommendation to any of you who are suffering from feelings of depression, loneliness, and worthlessness. Your energies are so heavy that your lifeforce energy is weak. You need to conserve it so we can help you build back your strength.

Besides, on the back of your eyelids, you will discover and witness so many wonders. Visions, colors, and images are all amazing signs that provide a wealth of information. I was personally delighted once I realized that a certain series of colored patterns that appeared were reflecting the opening of the corresponding energy channels, medians or chakras, within. I now let the colors inform me of where my energy is within my body. Delightful, divine play.

However, what I just described is a far cry from where I began. I was so exhausted—and pissed that I wasn't even sure I wanted to keep trying anymore. Setting aside time for myself to meditate demanded some space. When my body got the message, it basically regarded meditation as nap time. If you sleep, then sleep. We are a sleep-deprived people, in a world where the lights are always on and we are on call 24/7. Hey! At least you are building the habit of setting aside self-care time for yourself, right? Be immensely happy about that. Slowly, you'll find yourself sitting upright again and ready to breathe deep into your core and practice. Sleep can be deeply healing for both body and spirit.

If you have been faithful to improving your focus on the breath, you will slowly become aware that your breath and your heartbeat begin to sync up into a rhythm. Respect this! Hold it sacred! Allow your body to flow with this internal rhythm. You are anchoring to your authentic being-ness. It is providing powerful healing. And, you are literally embracing your full self in so doing.

This is truly the beautiful sacred dance of the most intimate form, our energy dancing with our physical form. The Tibetan Buddhists have thangkas that have great imaginative displays of this divine dance being performed. The union of body and spirit—of our dual natures balancing. Very sacred and beautiful.

And, this experience of being united in body and spirit, is at the heart of the kundalini tantra meditation practices that mistakenly gave rise to all sorts of sexual misuse and misunderstanding in the past... even today.

So, when your breath and heartbeat harmonize, it is a very good sign that you are getting "in tune" with yourself. Don't worry about time constraints. We're talking about basic self-care. Engaging in small acts of self-love always opens new spaces for us to inhabit.

Forgive all things. Remember, it is You that you are learning to love, which means you need to forgive yourself and heal. Doing so will truly lighten your life and your world. This alone will alter your energy.

Sustained reflections on this principle alone are transforming.

Besides, it's the only practical thing to do.

Suffering is self-created. Our bliss—our joy—is the natural state of existence, of homeostasis and harmony. So, stop marinating in misery or repeating the story of what isn't working out. It's time to break out of our mental prison and return to ourselves. As long as you are holding onto some hurt or misery, it festers within and continues to interfere with and distort your ability to thrive harmoniously in your life. You would never put a sealed bandage on an open wound full of debris and germs—something you're wise to remember when you set out to heal your soul.

Twenty Three

✦

Meditation – Attune & Center

We return to where we began. The sage's advice to begin where we are echoes more meaningfully to us now. We have gained a better understanding of the "who," "what" and "how" of our humanity so that we could determine "where" we are on our evolutionary journey. This powerful insight gains us our center—and the critical perspective necessary to free ourselves to discover our authentic non-dual selves.

Here are key components to incorporate into your centering meditation practice:

♦ Preparatory Physical Activity – Begin with an enjoyable physical activity to clear away the daily stressors and anxieties that fill your mind, emotions, and body. After which, it is always beneficial to perform some gentle stretching to facilitate aligning the air, blood, and energy flow within your body before sitting down to meditate. Some days may require more than others. I would also recommend that after this more outwardly strenuous activity, you perform the simple centering movements of 5 Element qigong.

♦ Create Space – Your life is sacred. Your meditation is a sacred act of loving-kindness. Recognize this. You need to invite your spirit into your daily life. Honor this by spending a few minutes creating a ritual for your meditation practice. Lighting a candle, prepare a comfortable seat, draw the curtains, put up a DND on the door, and go offline. This sends a signal to your body that you will be attentive to your body and spirit. In my personal practice I light a candle and perform a ritual of honoring the five directions; facing each in turn with the strike of the singing bowl. I visualize ground zero, emptiness, as the center, the fifth direction. A most sacred space: You.

♦ Sit Comfortably – Ideally, you will come to a position that keeps your spine in alignment and your chest open. If you are bent or constricted, it will not only inhibit the flow of energy but air and blood flow. This is part of the reason for traditional methods instructing on specific poses. However, I know that if you begin where you are, in whatever physical condition you are in, your body will slowly realign itself and open constricted areas as your body and energies synergize. Observing these improvements as you progress will provide you with positive feedback about the subtle transformation that is taking place deep within you.

♦ Close Your Eyes – Human eyes are quite vulnerable to the glare and blue light of our modern world. We have become over-reliant on all that we see. You need to be your own best guide here. Some souls whose minds are most agitated and active may benefit by using a simple candle flame or an image of a blue flower, as the Buddhist use, to be a focusing object to help settle the mind from scattered and chaotic thought patterns. Please keep in mind that your eyes are under constant strain and you expend a great deal of energy on the use of this critical sense organ. Close them. Open eyes take in the external. Closed eyes allow for internal focus. Allow them to help you strengthen your inner awareness and alignment. Let the act of closing your eyelids be the signal that you are ready to give yourself permission to focus on You.

♦ Breathe – Your breath work begins with a simple exercise. Take a finger from your right hand to gently close your left nostril, and breathe deeply into your belly; hold and transition to your left hand to close the right nostril before releasing the held breath. Breathe in deeply through your right nostril now; hold and transition back to holding your left nostril before releasing. Perform this exercise back and forth between the two nostrils until you have completed three full inhalations and exhalations from each nostril. This begins the subtle work of gathering your internal energies for focus.

♦ Focus – Having opened your air channels, find your natural breath. Most of us breathe from the chest. This is shallow and keeps the body in stress mode. For this reason, we should adopt an initial practice of focused breathing to re-habituate ourselves to the healthy, calming breath-work that was once natural to us as children. Deep belly breathing is very grounding. Counting breaths can also assist in holding your attention to effectively monitor your breathing pattern to ensure you go deep and slowly.

♦ Attune and Center – You are here to calm your agitated mind and settle the energies within you. As you breathe, it slows naturally, and your body begins to relax. Turn your focus to "feeling" your center core. Your heartbeat and your breathing. Let go of visualizing or focusing mentally. Allow your mental awareness to become an "empty" space. Let the mind quiet while you simply feel the energies, allowing the stresses and scattered thoughts to slip away from you. This does not happen immediately. You will catch yourself getting caught by some thought or emotion. When you do, simply thank yourself for becoming aware of this and return to perform focused breathing again. Catching yourself builds proficiency with each occurrence. So don't be frustrated when it happens. It's not nick names Monkey Brain for nothing! True centering is accomplished when you feel acute mental awareness yet remain empty of thought.

Although you will be adopting exercise and breath work in your daily activities, when it comes to a dedicated meditation session, one should aspire to gain for themselves a healthy fifteen or twenty minutes within the attune and centering portion of your meditation practice.

I'm a Little Teapot ...

... or a shapeshifting origin story

Born in the home of the Goddess of Bounty,
fully embraced by the city of angels;
born under a scorpion sky,
Fixed waters with vata energy—
an earthling of water and air.
A firstborn to parents
Fear and Anger.

My being of water and air
inside of fire and darkness
grounded upon Earth.
I was Water for Fear:
deepening the darkness, fulfilling her need.

I was Air for Anger
as fuel for fire,
feeding his need.

Yet ...
water and air inside fire's darkness? ah,
I'm a kettle—
Let's boil!

Nature and condition met, embraced, and merged,
a birth to transform, rise up as steam
into the light,
dissipation's rainbow,
to return
as rain again,
to calm and soothe
both fire and darkness,
fulfilling the need.

Fire's glow now caressing across the puddle
upon darkness' wound.
To heal yourself;
love yourself.
Your healing heals the world.

Twenty Four

✦

Meditation – Purify & Heal

This book is a vehicle to expedite your path into your inner journey to discovering your true self. I hope it helps to facilitate your remembering. May this book offer you a means to light your way through your darkness into the Light of your authentic being.

Here are a few key components to incorporate healing into your reflective meditation practice:

♦ Center Yourself Within – You are both a Light being of non-duality and a physical being of duality. Your centering meditations will progress to a point where you will feel your energies and body harmonizing into its internal rhythm and your mind has quieted down from its rampant discursive dialogue. When you reach a measure of stability in this quietude and calm, you will also begin to discern the difference between a scattered unbidden thought from your daily activities that is distracting from a thought that arises from the quiet prompting of your true being. Your body is beginning to open up, so you can begin the journey of discovering and healing You. Always conduct the reflective insight meditation after you have thoroughly established your being through the initial calm-abiding, centering meditation.

- ◆ Tonglen – The traditional method of tonglen is a visualization practice of recognizing the pain of others, taking it within you, filling it with love, and returning it with your exhalation, thus removing negative energy and sending out positive energy.
- ◆ Purification—My young life was marked with difficulties. I experienced immediate and present fear and violence. I knew I needed to find some means to center within myself: for survival, for strength, for nurturing, and for peace. I didn't know about meditation. I was a child. I called it "truth." "Just breathe the truth," was one of my mantras, at the time.
  - It was a place that allowed some relief from physical wounds... almost. "Since I am already hurting, and I can do nothing else but suffer through this," my child's mind reasoned. "Then, I will dedicate this to all others so that no one else ever needs to." This was my way of being brave—a warrior.
  - So this, then, became my practice: one of centering, then of purification—burning away my hurts and fears. And of walking. I was always in movement rituals, walking... and chanting... and crying... and laughing... and dancing... and singing. Very tantric! I am only highlighting the origin of using one's own pain and fear as fuel. This is the core of a purification practice that is healing. This is where you bring all frustrated energy. Burn it here. Our world is so aggressive and we hold so much fear and anger within us, I would recommend utilizing this type of purification in our meditation practices.
  - I mentioned earlier, I just became aware of an ancient form of very powerful purification practice which has since been codified by the Tibetan Buddhist as Chöd. Its origins connected to the impermanence of life and death, with rituals and healings performed in cemeteries and such like. So, I now observe how my adult shattered life took me on this odyssey to bring me full circle, back to my

centering and healing practices of a child. Witnessing my body's healing from the inside out has been a revelation. Knowing that you and I are no different, I'm certain that you, too, can do the same.

- Recognize and acknowledge this collective suffering; utilize what whatever is here as a means of healing the body and spirit. Use your own personal pain—your congested, blocked energy—to fuel a targeted look at how you process your thoughts, assumptions, and emotions. Allow yourself to grieve, and forgive yourself and the rest of the human family for the suffering we have inflicted upon ourselves in our ignorance. This is a critical element of forgiving others and breaking down barriers between you and others, especially those that you formerly "held" responsible for your wounds. You may not need any prompting, but oftentimes at the beginning of our interior journeys, there is so much that begs for our attention, so much pain and turmoil that it is difficult to parse. It overwhelms us, stopping us from venturing inward. Thus the equalizing effect of this book has been to help you cut through the outward layers of our shared confusion so you can focus on discovering the real You underneath.

♦ Mantra – I strongly encourage you to chant, recite, sing, and/or perform mantras. Be mindful of the affirmations you select and for what purpose. Habituate affirming, positive, uplifting energy and space within you to help break old paradigm thought patterns. Regarding one's own personal playlist, I would recommend that you spend some time reviewing them for the messages and emotions they invoke in you. Understand them before using them as a mantra form.

♦ Purify – When you are in a state of calm-abiding and the mind is no longer distracted, there will invariably arise a prompting from deep within you. Your body is beginning to trust and open up. Discern its nature. Focus on the energies and emotions, not on analyzing the minutiae of the he-said-she-said or he-did-this-she-did-that. Go behind the actions and words, and focus on the energies, which will help you cut through and discover the true nature of your imbalance and how you got yourself "off-center" to begin with. Invariably, this will lead to a wealth of surprises and self-discovery.

♦ Heal – You have already suffered and punished yourself, so your task is to name the hurt, acknowledge it and forgive yourself. Purification requires a great deal of love and patience to allow you to forgive yourself for being human. You are detaching and releasing yourself from the old paradigm's dualistic view of the world. Yes, it hurts, beyond all-knowing, but it is critical to embrace it, embrace yourself, and grieve wholeheartedly. Ideally, you will grieve until you are able to laugh at the foolishness of it all. When you can laugh through your tears, you know you have broken through for the healing to begin. This will free you to see and discover what it is that will truly make you happy. You will discover hidden aspirations, untapped talents, and unrecognized gifts that were always there within you. The more you trust this process, the more amazed and delighted you will be to the opening of your true nature and purpose. A return to your true source, your power, and your center will follow.

Twenty Five

Enlightenment

Buddhist monk Thích Nhất Hạnh once said, "Many people are alive but don't touch the miracle of being alive." Our world is undergoing great turbulence and change. If there is one thing that living with such uncertainty is teaching us, it is that this life of ours is a very precious gift. We are becoming more keenly aware that it is important to make the most of each and every moment of this precious life that is granted to us.

This is why you embarked upon this journey of self-discovery! True happiness, well-being, and prosperity depend upon bringing harmony to both aspects of our being: our physical and our energy bodies. To heal what hurts inside so that we can free ourselves to actually live more authentically, more joyously.

This is the time to realign with your intentions and who you truly are. You are where you are meant to be. This is the space for remembering, purging, healing, and opening yourself to grow into a wholeness that brings your body and soul together into balance. This is your transformation to rebirth yourself so that you can thrive. Allow this spiritual journey to dismantle the faux you, so you can find the authentic You underneath all that "nothingness". This is your life! It is precious. The gifts within you are precious... and those are the true you! Reveal your Light and thrive.

Remember, you are joyous Light! You are joy seeking expression. Your purpose is joy: homeostasis and resultant harmony! You are love and joy and freedom and clarity expressing itself.

So breathe. Relax. This is your spiritual journey. You are seeking your Light. Joy!

~~~~~~~

Twenty Six

Final Notes

USE this book! It's a guide. It's a meditation practice. It's a means to strengthen your more holistic, non-dual perspective. It was written as a purification exercise. As an active form of healing meditation, this practice is meant to help facilitate your self-discovery and healing. It has called upon you to listen with your heart and trust...

Trust that there is another way of being—one where you can heal your body and spirit—where you are actually happier and healthier, free to discover who you truly are and what it is that makes you Light up! It is time to embrace your divine nature and bring homeostasis to your body and spirit, matter, and energy. It's time to remember and become fully empowered humans as we were meant to become.

Anyone who has read my poetry, stories, and discourses is well aware that my writing is a distillation. There is so much contained within the content—almost more information contained between the lines than on them! Finding Your Light is no different. So, as you progress in your self-discovery, reading back through the book will reveal more that you may not have gathered in the initial reading. There is nothing hidden from you, just avenues of inquiry and depth of understanding to be acquired.

So, please let this book help you transform your life from the old paradigm of duality to a more authentic, holistic, non-dual view of your true nature as I have done. May this book offer you a means to light your way through your darkness into the Light of your true being-ness.

Finally, a thank you. It has been a privilege to embark on this journey with you. It is the same journey that I travel on and flourish. It has led me to you. May this book light your way. Many blessings to you! Radiate your joy—and Light!

Twënty Şëvën

✥

And for Thoşë Jntërëştëd: A Përşonal Rëfërral

After sending off this manuscript to my editor for review, I got an invitation to receive the White Tara empowerment. This is the Vajrayana Buddhist's highest form of practice for the female emanation of Avalokiteshvara or Chenrezig, the Buddha of Compassion.

While attending this event, I had an opportunity to spend a few hours sharing a meal with two women with whom I had a real connection. To be honest, I was terribly concerned about both of them, so I saw this as a wonderful opportunity to actually be in their physical presence and offer healing, visit, and eat together. Well, at one point, something I said triggered one of them to say that I sounded like her qigong master. She added that he did these Zoom classes designed for healing... Wow!

The universal energies work in amazing ways! She was right! A wonderful world indeed! I mean, this happenstance of a Buddhist practitioner that I reached out to from a different city—a different country—to just make an offhand comment that proved to be a most delightful gift and a resource! Well, as they say, all things come full circle. (Ha, what a perfectly Taoist thing to say!)

Her qigong master and I do very much speak the same language! And his 5 Elements movement practice as well as the other movements contained in his healing training videos do, indeed, appear within my own personal practices. So, for anyone who wishes to enhance the alignment of their physical and energy bodies, a perfect place to begin would be to check out the online offerings of Master Chunyi Lin, Spring Forest Qigong. As I am writing this into the book at the final editing stage before being printed, please know that I have not yet had a chance to let Master Lin know of this referral. He knows nothing of it. The true beneficiary of this happenstance is not mine or his, for that matter, but, rather, yours if you so choose.

If you do, then know that once you are connected and centered using these kinds of movements, you help yourself to become more fully your own compass. You can then later, more easily identify the type of yoga that you might wish to engage in if you find your body needs additional strengthening—especially for muscle and balance. Yoga offerings are vast and varied, from movement sequences to individual poses for working with specific channels.

Please listen to your body; slow down your body; slow down your mind. Be gentle. Your body needs quiet, subtle, internal body-energy alignment work. You may not think so. You and mind are living in a world of constant stimulation and always in a rush. Remember, you have let your mind run loose for a long time. So ignore that call to always be on the go. Allow the slower movements of these practices and poses to massage your muscles, massage your organs and tissues; let them stretch your veins and arteries, your ligaments, your thoughts. Combined with other forms of exercise like walking, dancing, jogging, a centered focus movement ritual like qigong and a healthy sitting meditation session is the perfect life-style format for total self-care and self-love! And, as a bonus, it's also a diet plan! I will end by saying that I am merely a conduit and just passing along this referral on behalf of White Tara. Many Blessings to you!

Om, Tare!

OM

Tara Tuttare Ture Soha!
I offer my humblest supplication our divine Light
That which simply IS
and to
Tara for giving me voice to light the way
that dispels fear and anger in this world.

Prayër for all thë Pëoplë

At this very moment, for the people and nations of this earth
May not even the names of disease, famine, war, and suffering be
heard. But rather, may pure conduct, merit, wealth, and prosperity
increase, and may supreme good fortune and well-being arise!

(A traditional Tibetan Buddhist prayer, often uttered, even by
H.H. Dalai Lama, and can be found on Lungta prayer flags.)

About The Author

When Elizabeth found herself rising up through the clouds only to discover she was standing naked in the middle of a pristine lake, caught in the beam of the bright full moon sitting at the left shoulder of Mt. Meru in a very, dark, still night, she knew that her life would never be the same again. Informed that all her dreams would come true for the mere task of solving a simple riddle. What she discovered...and remembered...will change your life.

After thirty plus years as a corporate professional advocating diversity, Elizabeth turned her energies to pursue creative and artistic ambitions. This was cut short. What follows is the true rendering of an extraordinary, yet quite ordinary, life of an empath, poet, visionary, who guides us through a spiritual transformation that unfolds the whole of the human family through history like an archeological dig through a physics prism. With a stroke of her pen, Elizabeth sweeps away the nonsense and fearlessly dares to tell us what we already know, and challenges us to love ourselves and dare to shine our Light.

Made in the USA
Monee, IL
21 October 2022

5bcae1ce-7ee9-43ee-adff-66d5c8114613R01